Sun Conure

Sun Conures as pets

Sun Conures Keeping, Pros and Cons, Care, Housing, Diet and Health.
by

Roger Rodendale

D1525326

Contents

Table of Contents

Table of Contents

Introduction

Sun Conures are one of the most beautiful birds that you could have at home as a pet. These gorgeous orange flushed birds that usually go by names like "Sunshine" or "Mango", make amazing pets as they are friendly and really social birds.

Bringing home a pet bird requires a completely different kind of preparation in comparison to other pets like a dog or a cat. These creatures are a lot more vulnerable and will take time to form a bond with people. Sun Conures are known to get extremely attached to just one or two members of the family and will even nip at others who try to handle them.

Well, overall, if you are the pet's parent, you are sure to fall in love with your Sun Conure just by the sight of these wonderful birds. These tropical birds love playing with people once they have formed a good and a strong bond with them. It is not just about the play, there are several other reasons why these birds make particularly amazing pets.

In general, birds make very intelligent pets. They are curious and so good at learning new things that you can expect a lifetime of fun with these creatures if you are able to give them a loving home. Train them to perform tricks and sometimes, even talk. That way, Sun Conures and most birds will make great pets to keep at home.

With our lifestyles forcing us to stick to apartments, it may be unfair to bring home larger pets that require more time outdoors. For those who love to add pets to their family, a bird like the Sun Conure may be the perfect one. Of course, you cannot have them cooped in the cage all day, but birds that are domesticated will love to move around the house and do not really require to be taken outside. In those terms, managing them becomes a lot less stressful. Even when you are out for several hours a day, you don't have to worry about where to keep them. They are great by themselves for a few hours, given that they have enough toys to play with.

The only concern is when you are a beginner at being a bird parent. They are more complex creatures and can be quite vocal and demanding from their owners. Remember that Sun Conures and all birds simply love the attention. And, they will make sure that you give it to them. So, if you are a person with a busy schedule, a bird is not as easy an option as it seems.

Growing up with pet birds has made me realize that they need to be raised in a social environment where they have someone to play with for at least a few hours a day. It is quite sad that people bring home Sun Conures just because these birds are really pretty and assume that they do not need too much care.

It is true that they are easier to take care of in comparison to dogs or cats. For starters, you don't have to clean up after them every time they poop. But other than that, there are various other things that you have to pay attention to. Like we discussed before, these creatures are highly intelligent and require a good amount of mental stimulation in order to be healthy. If you cannot give them that, you must definitely reconsider bringing the pet home in the first place.

When you are thinking about the Sun Conure, remember that you are thinking of the most popular pet species in the world. That may give the impression that these birds are not really "exotic". Hence their care must be easier and cheaper. But, think again. Are these birds native to the place that you live in? If not, then they are exotic creatures and you have to make sure that you are able to provide them with an ambience that they will thrive best in. You need to pay attention to the temperature, the water needed, the kind of food that will help them grow best and several other small and large things.

Ultimately, what you can be sure of with the Sun Conure is great assistance from other pet owners as there are many across the globe. That way, you have a better support system in comparison to other bird species. Sun Conures make great pets for beginners but you must make sure that all your research is in place if you are a new bird parent.

This book is a compilation of my experiences and the experiences of several fellow Sun Conure owners. These birds have such unique personalities that it is impossible to generalize behavior and care. Of course, there are a few basics that you can think about, but you need to know that your learning curve with these birds is never ending. You will always have something interesting to witness and learn about their behavior or even their general well-being.

This book covers some major guidelines that will help you bring a Sun Conure home and make him comfortable there. All the necessary tips about feeding, training and care have been covered in this book based solely on personal experiences.

The idea is to make sure that you are thorough with the:

- ✓ Origins and basic nature of these species
- ✓ Specific aspects of care such as feeding
- ✓ Behaviour of this bird
- ✓ Advantages of bringing one home
- ✓ The disadvantages of bringing one home
- ✓ Best way to bring home a healthy pet
- ✓ Medical needs of this species

When you have the basics in place you can understand if this pet is really the perfect option for you or not. If that is not enough to get you thinking about your priorities and deciding if you want this pet or not, you might find it interesting to know that these birds live up to 30 years of age. So add 30 to your current age and decide if will be able to keep the commitment for that long. If you are sure that you can, then this book is the perfect companion in the beautiful journey that you are about to begin with your pet.

Chapter 1: The Sun Conure

Sun Conures or lovingly known as "suns", are the most spectacular birds that you will ever see. These birds are extremely popular as pets simply because they are the most easily available conures in the world. Therefore, for several years, they have been considered the ideal companion birds because they also have wonderful personalities. In this chapter, we will learn a little about the species and its behavior.

a. **Physical Appearance**

Sun Conures, Sun Parakeets or Yellow Conures are medium sized birds that have been named the best looking parrots among the neo-tropical ones. A fully grown Sun will usually measure up to 30cms and will weigh about 120g. The long pointed tail is the trademark of this species and is quite a contrast to the medium sized bodies. But, the most remarkable trait of these birds is their plumage that comes in the brightest possible colors.

Coloration

The body of these birds is bright yellow in color overall. Distinct red markings are present on the lower abdomen, the lower back, the rump and the forehead. The area under the tail or the coverts are colored yellow and green just like the mantle and the wing coverts of the bird. You will see a bright shade of green in the secondary coverts. Then, in the outer parts of the main coverts you will see bright blue coloration. This means that you will notice the blue color only at the tips. If you are new to the world of birds, you need to know that "coverts" refer to the set of feathers in a designated part of the body. For instance, ear coverts are the feathers that cover the ears of the bird.

The tail is just as magnificently colored as the rest of the body. The upper part of the tail has an olive coloration and maintains the blue tips. The underside of the tail on the other hand is a mix of olive and gray.

The eyes of the bird have a distinct white outline with a contrasting dark brown pupil. The same dark coloration is noticed even on the legs and the bill of the bird. They will usually be a certain shade that lies between black and gray. In case of birds that are older, the feet have a sort of flesh tone to them.

You will see that the juveniles are a lot duller than the mature birds. They will have a larger amount of green feathers on the body, head and the throat. The bills are also lighter in color. The distinct orange-red markings on the breast, back, rump and abdomen are also poorly defined in the younger birds, until they reach the age of 18 months or even 2 years. In captivity, this change will take much longer and the birds seem to stay dull for long periods of time.

Males v/s Females

The above mentioned characteristics are with respect to the male birds. Although females do not look very different from the males, you will notice some obvious differences. To begin with, females have tails that are shorter that the males. In males, the tail typically measures about 131 to 141mm on an average and in females it will be anything between 121 and 146mm. Like most birds, the males tend to be more brightly colored. The abdominal region and the face, especially, are very bright in case of the male conures. But, you cannot standardize this for conures. These birds vary largely in coloration and sometimes the females will look exactly like a male. This is one of the many reasons why sexing these birds requires the help of an expert.

There are a few noted anatomical differences that are not entirely reliable but are worth knowing. The females have a rounder head that is smaller in comparison to the males. The males, on the other hand have squarer heads that are flat. In fact, their heads look longer and rectangular from a side view while the females' heads will appear almost triangular with the beak forming the tip of that triangle.

These defined edges make the male birds look stronger and bigger in their build. The femininity of their counterparts comes from a more slender and narrow frame. In comparison to the male birds, females are much lighter and tend to have smaller beaks. They even differ slightly in the skeletal structure with the females having a greater distance in the pelvic bones. This of course is to help the females lay eggs when they attain sexual maturity.

b. Taxonomy

The Sun Conure was described in detail by Carl Linnaeus, "The Father of Taxonomy" in his book, *Systema Naturae*. All the parrots that he described in this book were placed in the genus Psittacus. However, there have been many changes in this system of taxonomy and the New World parrot species have been placed under the genus *Aratinga*. Today only African grey parrots fall under the former genus name.

The name of the Sun Parakeet consists of the epithet *Solstitialis* which in Latin means 'Summer Solstice'. Basically, this word which also means "Sunny" refers to the beautiful golden plumes of the Sun Conures. There are two widely accepted names of this species. Authorities like world renowned ornithologist, Thomas Arndt use the name Sun Conure. On the other hand, the American Ornithologists' Association recognizes these birds as the Sun Parakeet. Even in several field guides of birders and some official lists of birds, they are known as Sun Parakeet.

This species is considered monotypic meaning that there are no subspecies under it. However, some species from Brazil such as the JandayaParakeet, the Sulphur Breasted Parakeetand the Golden Capped Parakeet were considered to be subspecies of the Sun Conure. But, recently several other authorities contested that these birds are all from separate species altogether.

The Sulphur Breasted Parakeet and the Sun Conure in fact represent the same species apparently. This became a very important subject of discussion when the former came into recognition in the year 2005. Until then the bird was practically unnoticed because of its close resemblance to the Sun Parakeet. In captivity, the Suns, the golden capped Parakeets and the Jandaya Parakeets are interbred. Even in the wild, there are some cases of interbreeding between these species. However, authorities now believe that the juveniles of each species have been mistaken for hybrids while they actually are not. Largely, it is believed that these birds are allopatric. This means that due to several factors including geographic separation, it is not really possible for any genetic exchange between them. The Suns and the Sulphur Breasted Parakeets do come in contact in the Southern Guianas but it is not certain if there can be any hybrids between the two in the wild.

c. Range and Distribution

In terms of distribution, the Sun Conure can be seen almost all over the world because of their popularity as the ideal bird. However, naturally, these birds are usually abundant in the continent of South America. They occupy almost the whole of the continent, but thrive abundantly in the areas to the North of the Amazon River. This means that they are quite common in Brazil, especially in the Mount Roraima region and the Pacaraima Mountains. Their population extends from here all the way to Rio Branco including Para, Ampa and the Eastern part of the Amazonas.

Although there are no written or published records, these birds have rarely been spotted in Southern French Guiana close to Santa Elena in the southeastern part of Venezuela. This range is almost considered hypothetical because just one sighting was made in this region. Such rare sightings have also occurred in the region between Pomeroon River and the Guyana North. Until the 1970's these bids were quite common in Roraima and Guayana. However, these birds came under great trapping pressure and almost became absent in these regions.

Sadly, in other parts of Brazil such as the Mau river and the Contao Cotingo rover, these birds were abundantly only till the 1990s. Here, too, they perished because of the pressures of trapping. There are absolutely no recent records of these birds in these localities where they were so prominent. Even in the Maraca Ecological Station, they have stopped thriving post the year 2000. In some cases, they have also perished because of the unavailability of the habitat that they require. These localities are unable to support the dry forests that these species require to survive in.

Other common regions that they inhabit include the eastern and southern regions of Surinam and the savannahs of Sipaliwini. There is a good population to the south of the Amazon River as well. Some Conures are seen near the tributaries of the Amazon and also near the Canuma River and Santarem.

Interestingly, these birds that are native to South America, have also been observed in Florida quite recently near the Wilton Maner. Only two birds were seen here leaving a good chance for accidental or unintentional release. After all, they are a commonly seen pet in most parts of North America.

d. Habitat

The exact habitat of this species is not very clearly understood. The only certainty that researchers have about the habitat of this bird is that they are found only in tropical habitats. This includes open savannahs or the dry woodlands of the savannahs. The area along the banks of the Amazon river consists of scrublands that these birds are usually found in. Besides that, they also live in the coastal forests and some forests that are seasonally flooded.

Altitude plays a very important role in the habitat of these birds. They require altitudes less that 1200 meters. Therefore, some birds may also be found in the slopes of mountains or in the valleys. Regions that are rich in palm grooves are also a favorite habitat of the Sun Conures. They will be seen in regions with bushes and trees that have abundant fruiting.

The habitats of Sun Conures are not very well known simply because these birds have not been studied well in the wild. They are seen in some of the most underdeveloped parts of South America that are really hard to explore and study. As a result, the records available of the habitat are very limited.

One thing that has been observed in the few habitats that have been studied is that these birds tend to thrive in forest regions post forest fires. In the wild, they are extremely sensitive to any human activity and prefer to stay in areas that have less contact. So in the regions that have heavy cattle grazing, you will spot these birds quite rarely.

All in all, the Sun Conures inhabit a wide range of habitats across South America. They are purely tropical birds and all habitats that are common here like the savannahs or the semi deciduous forests, make good homes for the birds.

e. Food Habits

The food habits of Sun Conures in the wild are known very little. As mentioned before, there is less information about this bird in general considering their remote habitat. Most of the knowledge about the food habits of Suns comes from examinations conducted in the stomach contents of some specimens. These examinations revealed that the birds eat buds, blossoms, fruit pits, some wind dispersed seeds and even insects. These birds are also known to feed on Red Cactus along with legume pods and Malphigia berries.

The diet of the birds varies depending upon the season. For example, they need to have more protein in their intake in the breeding season. When they are rearing young birds or when they expect long flights such as the migration season, they need to stock up on energy. That is when the carbohydrate requirements of this species is high. Of course, when the young ones are developing or when the females are producing eggs, they naturally need to have more calcium in the food that they consume. In fact, these birds are known to adjust their diets when they need to.

In captivity, however, the dietary pattern of these birds is very different. They require a large range of foods from beans, nuts, grains, fruits, vegetables to seeds. But, what you need to know about Sun Conures is that they are massive bingers and will eat just about anything, even if it is not the food that will give them good nutrition. Therefore, it has been observed that most birds are highly malnourished in captivity. In some rare cases, owners have reported that their Conures simply loved to eat, and ate very well, and still died of malnutrition.

Strangely, these birds are not instinctive towards nutritious foods in captivity. They will eat just grass seeds as well. This has a very negative impact on breeding. One interesting food related behavior with respect to Sun Conures is that they eat foods that they are familiar with. When they are introduced to a new food, they will not eat it unless they have seen another bird eat it! They want to try new foods when they see someone else eat it. So, in captivity, they reach out for the foods that they have seen their owners eat. This is not a healthy habit and you must make sure that you discourage your bird when you see him or her nibbling at your plate.

f.   Behavior

Sun Conures are very social birds and tend to live in pairs in the wild. These birds are monogamous meaning that they have just one sexual partner all their life. They fly in flocks that have a strength of anything between 3 to 15 birds. In the wild, the most commonly observed flock is a group of 5 birds. In case of areas where bushes and fruit bearing trees are abundant, you may even find huge flocks of up to 30 birds!

The beauty of these birds is that they are loyal and extremely social. You will never learn of a Sun Conure who abandoned his flock. They do migrate seasonally or in search of food, but always stick to their own flock. In some parts, you will see Sun Conure populations in a particular area all year round.

Sun Conure flocks fly for long hours covering several miles every day. Note this point as it emphasizes on the fact that these birds need exercise to grow into healthy adults. They have a direct and swift flight and they merge beautifully into their rainforest backdrops despite their bright coloration. The flight of these birds is extremely noisy. The flocks are only quiet when they are feeding.

When they are about 5 months old, young Conures will find themselves a partner. In captivity, one strange behavior that has been noticed is that pairs of Conures of the same gender also behave like partners. You will see them feeding each other and even mating!

Baby Conures are very responsive to bright light. Before they open their eyes, they live in dark places and will react by trembling, flinching or even hiding from bright light. You must know that bright lights are harmful for the growth of baby Conures. It can make them blind or even lead to severe psychological stress. When they first open their eyes, Conures are nearsighted. They will always recoil and hide when they have a distant object before them. However, these birds develop their vision because of their innate sense of curiosity. They move towards objects around them, feel them and then develop their vision.

These birds are very impatient. You will learn this when you bring one home. Even as helpless little babies, they are eager to start flying even before they wean! They are stubborn to the extent that they stop eating and lose interest in food because all they want to do is fly.

These birds are usually quite calm and gentle except when they molt. This is an uncomfortable process and will make them very irritable. They are only calmed down when the humidity is increased or when they are given a warm shower. This makes the pin feathers open out easily, making them less irritable.

In terms of intelligence, these birds are at the top. They are highly curious and smart. They are constantly seeking some form of mental stimulation from their environment. When they are not able to do this, they are prone to developing behavioral problems such as chewing, biting and even screaming. Otherwise, when raised in a mentally stimulating environment, these birds learn to talk and manage to ace several tricks. They have the unique skill of manipulating their tongues, bills and feet.

Here are some key behavior patterns that you can observe in Sun Conures generally:

They are sedentary creatures in terms of their territory.
They are arboreal, meaning that they live in trees.
They are active during the day or are diurnal.
They are nomadic in their territory. In a defined territory, these birds like to keep moving around.
They are extremely social.

Ecological Role of Sun Conures

Sun Conures are popular seed dispersers. They can transport seeds from the parent plant to new locations, allowing the populations to increase. They eat the seeds and excrete them without any change in their stool. That is why, there is a huge threat to the ecosystem in places where Sun Conure populations have been damaged due to human activity. One area where the effects have been studied is in the population of the Mauritia palm tree that is native to South America. Sun Conures usually nest in these trees and because of a huge depletion in their population owing to trapping, the seeds of these trees are not transported anymore leading to reduced specimens of this species.

Similarly, in areas where the harvesting of the Mauritia Palm is excessive, Sun Conure birds not just reduce in numbers, but also lose their important function in the ecosystem which is seed dispersion of this tree.

g. Humans and the Sun Conures

Sun Conures are an important part of the economy. They are the primary source of income in the international pet trade. However, trading these birds is considered illegal as it is putting the population of this species at risk.

Sun Conures have been trapped and transported extensively in the Brazilian and Mexican regions. As a result, several infectious diseases have been exchanged between the captive and the wild populations. One of the most common diseases that is exchanged is Inclusion Body Hepatitis. Besides that, diseases like Dilatation Syndrome and Feather and Beak Disease have also been noticed among the ones that are exchanged as a result of transport.

They spread some deadly types of virus like Papovirus, Reovirus, Poxvirus, Adenovirus, Herpesvirus and Paramyxovirous among the human population. They can be spread by the eggs as well.

When Sun Conures are badly bred, there are also resultant deformities and illnesses among birds. These diseases and deformities put the popularity as well as the availability of these birds at risk for parrot lovers. This puts the thriving breeding business at risk.

One thing that makes these birds a negative factor includes damaging the crops that are grown within their range. It is also believed that the Ancient Mayan Civilizations moved out of their own villages in a desperate attempt to get away from these birds or other voracious species. They are known to cause extensive crop devastation.

h. Conservation Status

It is quite ironic that one of the most popular pet parrot species is actually endangered in the wild. Pet trade and illegal trafficking has led to a rapid decline in the number of Sun Conures found in the wild. The avian family, *Aratinga,* that these birds belong to is one of the most endangered in the world. Other factors that result in the decline of these species include loss of habitat and even hunting for their beautiful plumage. Only for pet trade, 800,000 Sun Conures are caught per year.

In the year 1992, a Wild Bird Conservation Act was passed to protect these birds. This banned the import of Conures into the United States. Most of the birds that you will find in this region have been bred in captivity purely for domestication. Even the European Union has banned the import of any bird from the wild since 2007. With these laws in place, there is some relief of the population of these birds.

Until 2004, these birds were placed under the least concern division by the IUCN. However surveys in Guyana and Brazil revealed that they have become lesser in number in these parts. In just 4 years, these birds were listed as Endangered in 2008 by the IUCN. After the laws, however, there is a decent increase in their number in Guyana. However, this increase is not enough to take them out of the endangered category.

Once you have decided that you should bring home a Sun Conure, the next thing you need to do is ensure that you are bringing the right bird home. With several species looking strikingly similar it is easy for a newbie to get confused. The next chapter lists the differences between the Sun Conure and similar birds in detail.

Chapter 2: Sun or Sunday?

If you are new to the world of parrots, it can be extremely confusing to pick the right species to bring home. While Sun Conures are the most popular, there are chances that you actually have an entirely different species that looks very similar. These birds differ largely in their care and other needs. So as the pet parent you should be sure of the species that your bird belongs to. Here are a few simple ways to distinguish between the Sun Conure and other species that it is usually mistaken for.

a. Sun Conure v/s Jenday Conure

These two birds share a lot in common and are considered to be two of the most popular parrot species that are kept as pets. Jenday Conures are also known as Sunday Conures so it is that easy to make a mistake when you are bringing a bird home.

The main distinguishing factor between the two birds is the plumage. Both the birds have a yellow head that is the cause of the confusion. But, if you look closely, Sun Conures have a larger proportion of yellow on their wings making them brighter in their appearance. On the other hand, the Jendays or the Sunday Conures are predominantly green in color. The top of the wings of the Sun Conure is colored in yellow with bright orange markings.

You will see only a small amount of red on the head and the belly of the Jendays. The eyes have a bright red color around them in case of the Sun Conures while the Jendays tend to have a very small bit of it. The ring just around the eyes is white in the case of the Suns and grey in case of the Jendays. This makes the former look a lot more attentive and bright.

Now, the habitat and range of the birds differ as well. Sun Conures are seen mostly in the north and western parts of Brazil while jendays are seen at the opposite end in the Southwestern portion. It is true that Sun Conures are a very poorly studied species. There is lesser known about the Jendays because of this.

The Jenday is not considered endangered unlike its cousin. The Sun Conures are threatened by depleting populations as well as trapping.

These birds have a lot of similarities as well. They are known for their ability to make very interactive pets. They display interesting behavior patterns and are very bold and curious creatures. The dietary requirements of both the birds are almost the same. They demand attention and can be quite noisy when they do not get that. When kept as pets, they both tend to require many toys, especially the chewable ones. These birds are very active and can be trained to perform an array of tricks. Now, it is difficult to get them to talk, but that is not a big concern considering how entertaining both Sun Conures and Jendays can be.

b. Sun Conure v/s The Green Cheeked Conure
In the wild, it is not hard to distinguish between the two because one is yellow and the other is green. However, in captivity, as a result of interbreeding, Green Cheeked Conures have also started to sport yellow and orange plumes just like the Sun Conure. Still, there are various factors that make it possible to distinguish between the two quite easily.

The vocalization volume is the main difference between the two. If you want a quieter bird, the green cheek is a better choice for you. Their vocalization is almost half as loud as the Sun Conure. In addition to that, they do not vocalize as frequently as the Suns. Sun Conures use their voice to indicate their location. This is not a common practice among the Green Cheeks. As a result, the latter is more suited for apartment lives.

Of course, there is a massive difference of the genus that these birds belong to. While the Sun Conures belong to genus *Aratinga,* the green cheeks are classified under the genus *Pyrrhura.* The former consists of colorful and attractive birds. The latter consists of green birds that are more soft voiced than the other.

They also differ in size. While both are medium sized birds, the green cheeks tend to grow up to 10 inches in length when fully mature. On the other hand, Sun Conures are a good 2 inches larger, measuring up to 12 inches. The Sun Conure is also stouter when compared to the Green Cheeks that tend to be slender. The beak of the Sun Conure is also relatively larger.

The behavior of these birds is very similar. They both love to play and are extremely clever birds. They simply love the idea of snuggling and cuddling. Of course, they are great attention seekers and will demand the attention of their owners. They tend to be screamers when they are not given enough attention.

Of course, they are both parrots that cannot be trained to talk too well. They may utter a few words at the most. Even this does not happen with a clear voice like other species of parrots. But that does not make them less interesting to their owners. You can train both species to perform various tricks as they are extremely fast learners. Their curiosity makes them great leaners.

c. Sun Conure v/s Golden Capped Parakeets

Sun Conures and Gold Capped parakeets are easy to distinguish because of the coloration. The Gold caps are predominantly green in color with yellow or bright markings on the top of their head. They are larger birds in comparison to the Sun Conures. While the latter will grow up to 12 inches, Gold Caps can be about 14 inches in size when fully grown. The tail feathers have a blue tip with the same coloration on the underwings and the primary feathers in case of the Gold Caps. In case of Sun Conures, these regions are all orange in color.

The eyes of both species have a beautiful white ring around them. In addition, the iris of the Gold Caps and the Sun Conures are usually brown. In comparison to the Sun Conures, the Gold Caps are far mellower and tend to be less vocal. They limit their screams to bedtimes, dawn and times of extreme excitement. While Gold Caps also require as much attention as the Suns, they do not become very vocal about it like the Suns.

Both birds are very social and friendly. They love to cuddle and play. The inability to learn to talk clearly is a factor that is similar between these two bird types as well. Of course, the trainability of Sun Conures and the Gold Caps is equally high, making them wonderful pets. They are quite active and can both become very acrobatic with training.

d. Sun Conure v/s Sulphur Breasted Parakeet

Both birds belong to the same genus and are believed to be closely related. Sulphur Breasted Parakeets are often mistaken to be juvenile Sun Conures. However, the inability of Sulphur Breasted Parakeets to molt into bright yellow colors when then are adults reveals their true identity. The orange markings of these birds reduce with maturity and form a mask on the face when they are fully grown. The body of these birds is mostly green while the Sun Conures are predominantly bright yellow in color.

The juveniles of both the species are significantly different in their appearance. In addition to that the wings of the Sulphur Breasted Parakeets are shorter in comparison to the Sun Conures. In general, Sun Conures are larger than Sulphur Breasted Parakeets. The latter can be about 10 inches in size while the former grows up to 12 inches and even weighs more.

The two birds differ in their conservation status. Sun Conures are endangered birds while Sulphur Breasted Parakeets are not. This is primarily because of their range in the wild Sulphur Breasted Parakeets live in the Monte Alegre region where trapping is not that big a concern.

In terms of personality, the two birds are extremely similar. They are both playful and social birds. Their high intelligence gives them the ability to learn several new tricks. Their curious nature makes them extremely interesting to watch and hence quite fun to have at home as your pets.

Chapter 3: Bringing a Sun Conure home

Sun Conures are exotic pets that are bred in captivity in places that are not native to them. This gives you various options to source your Sun Conure. Each one has its pros and cons. The only thing that matters is that the bird you bring home should be in good health. Only then will these birds be able to interact and socialize in their new environment.

a. Where Can You Find One?
There are three best options if you are looking at bringing a new bird into your family. Each has its own benefits and it is up to you to choose one that makes you comfortable.

Conure Breeders
There are several Sun Conure Breeders in all the areas where these birds are popular pets. You can find a breeder near your home by looking up websites like www.birdbreeders.com that carry listings of some of the most popular breeders in your locality. If you are not one who relies on internet searches, you can even ask a bird store owner to help you find one. You can even speak to fellow Conure owners to introduce you to the breeders that they work with.

The advantage of getting your birds from a breeder is that they are likely to be healthier. You see, most breeders will focus on one type or family of birds. They will spend a lot of time learning about them and putting together the best breeding practices to produce healthy babies. You have various scales at which people practice Conure breeding. Some of them just have a backyard breeding business and others choose to do this on a more professional level. Either way, you should be able to find a healthy bird if you find a good breeder.

Now, you have several breeders who will sell these birds through online stores. That is acceptable only if you are certain about the reputation of the breeder. Otherwise, it is recommended that you pay at least one visit to the facility to check the breeding conditions. There is one golden thumb rule when it comes to breeders: If the environment is clean, the birds will be healthy. Check how the cages have been maintained, see if there is clean water for the birds and also understand how much these breeders actually interact with their birds. That way you can be certain of not just a healthy bird, but also one that is social to some extent. Here are some handy tips when you are choosing a breeder to buy your bird from:

- **Check for their experience**. It is mostly suggested that you opt for breeders who have been in the business for a good amount of time. They will have experience with respect to various issues faced by bird owners and will become a valuable source of support for new bird owners. Of course, there may be some new breeders who are extremely passionate about their birds. In such cases, check for how much experience they have with managing and handling Conures, be it their own pets or pets of friends and family.

- **Check if they have an avian veterinarian**. This is very critical. Every good breeder will be associated with an avian veterinarian. That is how they are able to have the birds regularly examined to give you some guarantee on their health. If the breeder does not have an avian veterinarian that he or she can recommend, you may want to look for new options immediately.

- **The breeder must follow the closed aviary concept**. That way you can be sure that the birds that come to your home will be disease free. -

- **Check the breeder's website**. If you have come to know of a breeder through an email or a flyer, you must check for a website immediately. All good breeders will have one and will tell you in detail about their breeding practices on these websites.

- **Look for recommendations**. This is undoubtedly the best way to find a reliable breeder. You can ask the breeder if you can talk to other Sun Conure owners that he or she deals with just to understand how they have been able to cope with the bird. In the process, you will know if the owner and the breeder share a good relationship or not. If the breeder is hesitant to connect you to their customers, it is a sign of something fishy.

A breeder who truly looks out for his birds will also be a valuable part of raising your Conure. He or she will be able to help you with all the initial preparations that you need to make in order to welcome your pet Conure home. Along with a vet, your breeder is the only support you will need to raise a healthy bird in your home.

What is a Closed Aviary Concept?

This is a common practice among most bird breeders to ensure that the birds are free from any diseases. They follow strict quarantining rules to prevent any germs from entering their flock and damaging the health of the birds. There are a few rules that are followed with the closed aviary:

1. Usually, new birds are not added to the flock: In case there is a need to add a new bird for whatever reason, they make sure that it is quarantined for a minimum period of 3 months and a maximum of 6 months.

2. The birds that are taken to the vet are quarantined too: Now, the chances of catching infections and diseases are maximum at the vet. So, breeders quarantine them to ensure that they do not bring back any airborne viruses. Even at the vet, these birds are usually covered with large towels to reduce the risk of infections.

3. They keep all birds out of the premises: That means they do not allow their friends, customers or anyone bring birds in. Even rescues are not permitted unless there is a chance to quarantine them first.

4. They do not go to any place where there are other birds: This includes pet stores and even bird shows. They definitely do not take their birds there. And, in an event when they themselves go to one such event, they will take a shower and change their clothes fully before handling their own aviary. They do this to ensure that there are no chances of any indirect contact resulting in infections.

Breeders with these practices can be trusted as they invest a lot of energy to keep the health of their birds at its peak.

Pet Stores
You will be able to find several specialty stores that deal with birds alone. These are the most preferred source for your Sun Conure. Most such pet stores have a lot of information about the birds that they are selling. This will make the process of bringing a new pet home much easier for new owners. You need to enquire about the history of the bird that you choose just to be clear that the pet store has enough information about what they are selling you. They should be able to tell you a little about the general behavior of the bird, its parent and even a little about the breeder who they deal with.

Examine the conditions that these birds are living in very carefully. If you see that the cages have not been cleaned well and the water contains feathers of bird droppings, it is an indication that the bird may be unhealthy. This also shows that they have not been given enough attention which is a sure sign of behavioral problems. Ask if the pet store will offer any sort of health certificate. Some of the good stores will be able to give you a minimum guarantee on their pets.

It is alright to bring a bird home from the regular pet stores as well. As long as they have been cared for, you have nothing to worry about. When dealing with pet stores, you may want to do a little research about them and even shop around a little before you finalize a bird for yourself.

Conure Parent Tip: In case you plan to have a Sun Conure shipped to you, whether from a breeder or an online pet store, ask for the following:

- ✓ *Pictures of the specific bird that you are going to get. Close ups and several angles are a must.*
- ✓ *A valid return policy in case the bird does not meet the right health expectations.*
- ✓ *Testimonials from clients and also a possible chance of interacting with them.*

Adoption

Rescue shelters are often filled with several varieties of Conures. Since Sun Conures are common pets, you are most likely to find them in these shelters. Adopting is one of the best options because it is extremely noble. You are giving a bird a chance at a second life. Most of these birds may be ill-treated, abused or injured. And, they need a loving home. But, adoption is an option if you are sure that you have the experience to handle the needs of unhealthy birds or even birds with behavioral problems.

In case you are not able to do that yourself, you should at least have the assistance of a fellow Conure owner. These birds may also be expensive to take care of as they will require special medical assistance. Of course, they need your undivided attention in order to be able to recover fully. If you think you can provide that, adopt a Sun Conure instead of buying one.

b. Ask for Health Certificates

A breeder should give you a health certificate for your bird and most pet stores do the same too. But, what is a health certificate and how does it help a bird owner?

A health certificate or guarantee is a document that assures of the health of your bird. For birds like the Conures, you will normally receive a 90 day health guarantee. This states that if you find any health issues in the bird in 90 days or less, you can return it to the breeder or the store. A health guarantee is a symbol of very good animal husbandry practices. It shows that your breeder or pet store is willing to commit to the health of your pet.

These certificates require you to have your Sun Conure examined by an avian veterinarian within 72 hours, i.e. 3 days of purchase. If your vet determines that there are health conditions, even genetic conditions, that are cause for concern, you will be able to return your bird. You will have to present a written document from the vet that confirms the problems with the health of the Conure. Once that is done, you will be able to either exchange the Conure or get a full refund.

Health Guarantee Conditions:

Every health guarantee comes with a set of conditions that you need to be aware of:

You HAVE to get the bird examined in 72 hours by an avian vet. Usually, there are a list of vets who are approved by the aviary and it is best to go to them. This cost for this examination will be paid by you.

Any illness that may be caused because of poor conditions provided by you in the 90 days period are not covered. Stress related illnesses are not covered in guarantees.

In case of any environmental condition or other circumstances like a fire or smoke that may cause health problems to the bird, you cannot avail this guarantee.

They do not cover for any veterinarian costs incurred in these 90 days.

Behavioral problems will not be considered by the health guarantee.

It is best that you learn about choosing healthy Conures before you actually make the purchase. That way, you will avoid the stress of exchanging or returning the birds. There are some easy ways to identify an unhealthy or sick bird or a bird with possible health issues.

c. Baby or Adult?

The next pressing question is at what age should you ideally bring the bird home? Should it be an adult or do you think you can handle a baby? Let us go through the pros and cons of each and you should be able to make that decision instantly:

Bringing a baby Conure home

A baby Conure like any other baby bird is quicker to adapt to its new home. They will take a few hours to get used to the place that they have to live in for the rest of their lives. A baby Conure will look different from the adult in coloration. They tend to have a higher proportion of green feathers. Usually, it is recommended that pet parents hand feed the babies. That way, you will be able to form a stronger bond with them. Baby Conures will pick up behaviors that you teach them easily and it is also easier to correct any inherent behavioral problems like biting in case of a baby bird.

You need to remember, however, that a baby bird is more delicate and you need to be extremely careful when it comes to handling them. They also need to be observed very closely for the first two days, especially if they have been newly weaned. You need to handle them for short periods of time regularly to get them used to you. In addition to that, you also have to keep an eye on the feeding habits and the droppings of the Conure. If you notice any abnormality, it may be a warning sign for an impending health

30

issue. At around 10 months of age, these birds molt and grown new plumes. That is a stressful period and can make them very nippy. Some Conure owners will tell you that this stage is very hard to handle.

Bringing an adult Conure home

You are most likely to bring home an adult from a rescue shelter. A Conure who has crossed puberty is called an adult. That is around the age of 2 for most of them. When you bring home an adult Conure that has been socialized or is used to handling, do not assume that you will have an easy task with the bird. Conures do get attached to their owners, but may only get attached to one or two people at a time. The best thing about an adult is that you are aware of the personality. Depending on that you may figure out how to get him to adapt.

So when you remove a Conure from his environment, he will be under a lot of stress. This induces behavior like screaming and nipping. A bird that is stressed is also scared. That is why you may find it hard to handle him or her. But with some care and a reasonable adjustment period, you should be able to tame the adult Conure. We will talk about this in greater detail in the next few chapters.

The benefits of bringing an adult home is that they are stronger than and not as delicate as the little ones. Once they have gotten used to your home, you may discover that they already know a couple of tricks that are interesting.

It does take some experience to care for an adult. If you are a first time parrot parent, you may want to think about bringing a baby home as it is simpler.

Conure Parent Tip: You can bring home a pair of Sun Conures if you like. But, if you want your bird to form a bond with you, it is best that you bring just one home. With two birds, it is likely that they will form a bond with each other. If you do not have a lot of time for your Conure, bring home a pair for sure.

Although some breeders would suggest that a single female is gentler than the male, the truth is that there is hardly much difference. It depends entirely on the temperament of each bird and you may choose to bring home a female or a male and train them to blend into your family.

d. Knowing if the Conure is Healthy

Whether you are bringing a Sun Conure home form a breeder or a pet store, you need to know if the bird is healthy or not. Here are some definite signs of poor breeding practices. If you see any of these signs or symptoms, there is a good chance that the bird you bring home will not be healthy:

- The nares of the Conure should be dry. Nares are the Nasal cavity of the bird. If you see any mucus or wetness, it is a sign of infection.

- If you have a chance of handling the bird, feel the body. There should not be any lumps. You must especially check the underside of the wings and the belly for any such lumps.

- Typically, a Sun Conure is stout, but not plump. If you see excess weight on the body of the Conure that you choose, you need to be concerned.

- Conures are active birds. If they are lethargic or do not react immediately upon seeing you approach their cage it is a sign of some behavioral problem or some issue in the eating habits of the bird.

- Make sure that the Conure has an erect posture. That is a sign of good skeletal development which is essential for the bird's health.

- The eyes should be clear and not puffy and watery. This is also a sign of infection.

- When you are looking at bringing a chick home, it is essential that their feathers are not damp and ruffled. This is a sign of poor sanitation and husbandry.

- Check the legs and the feet. The skin on it should look healthy.

- In case of any bird, the beak is the first sign of health. If there is any damage to the beak or any abnormality, you need to check with a vet.

These are the first signs of health with respect to the Conures. However, the first two days of bringing the bird home are the most critical ones. This is when you will discover how healthy your bird is.

e. Bringing them home, literally!

Alright, so you have a healthy bird that you picked and you absolutely love him. But, the challenge is how do you bring him home? Your breeder or the pet store should be able to help you with that. However, this is a critical piece of information that pet buyers do not think about. You should be able to get a large collapsible box at the breeders' or at the pet store. Sometimes you may have to buy them separately. So, that is something you need to be prepared for. If you have a large and clean cat carrier, even that should help you

Conure Parent Tip: Ask where your bird has been bred? Is it HANDBRED or AVIARY BRED? Most Conure enthusiasts will confirm that aviary bred birds are almost impossible to train although the pet store owner may tell you otherwise. Unless you buy the bird at a very young age, you should not opt for aviary bred ones.

Chapter 4: The Sun Conure is Home!

You have taken the leap and brought a Sun Conure home. As a new parent, you may find the preparation a little overwhelming. But, if you take it step by step, you should be able to make this transition easy for the bird and less stressful for you.

The only thing that you need to prepare is a large enclosure that will become the bird's home. Add a few parrot toys into the cage. You should include a water bowl and a food bowl. Try to keep the cage really large. Ideally, the cage should be about 24"X24"/30". This will let them flap their wings about and will keep them comfortable.

Place this enclosure in a room that is not too busy. It should also be relatively quiet. So if you can hear a lot of traffic or if there is too much sunlight in a certain room, this may not be the best place for the Conure to spend his first day in. It needs to be a quiet room that you will be moving around in, preferably.

a. Preparing your Family

It is natural for people to want to play with the Sun Conure. After all, it is such a pretty bird and everyone will want to put their fingers through the cage and try to fondle the bird. This will stress him out a lot. So, it is a good idea to lay down a few guidelines to the family when you bring a new Sun Conure home:

1. Leave the bird alone. Everyone should be asked to refrain from approaching the cage, tapping on it or crowding around it.

2. Do not talk to the bird. This is the most important instruction. Saying hello in different voices is more stressful than you can imagine for your Sun Conure.

3. Do not introduce new people to the house and allow them to play or approach the bird. You see, a Sun Conure, as beautiful as it is, is not an object that you want to show off. It is a bird that can get really scared and develop health issues with stress.

4. No pictures and selfies! The flash from your camera or even the sound made by the camera can be a trigger for aggressive behavior. You will always have several opportunities to take pictures of the Conure. Just be sure that you do not do that on the first day of the bird's arrival into your home.

5. No loud music. On the first day, especially, the Conure needs a lot of calm and quiet. Keep him in a room that has less traffic noises.

6. Do not slam doors shut. Sudden noises are not appreciated by Sun Conures. They are really frightened by these sudden and loud noises.

7. No large or colorful toys near the cage. This can also aggravate the stress for your bird. Children do things like taking their teddy bears close to the cage and saying, "Boo!" This should never be done. Not the first day or any other day.

8. Prepare your family for the fact that your Sun Conure can be a screamer. He may scream all night long. This is his way of displaying fear. He may also be calling out to the other birds in the aviary or to his previous owner. It will subside if you do not disturb the bird and keep him calm.

9. Do not feed the bird from your hands on the first day. In fact, you need to tell them not to approach the cage with

treats for a few days. This may induce biting or nipping as the birds go straight for the fingers. And if someone shouts or screams when he does this, the bird feels encouraged!

10. No one will handle the bird. Even the most experienced bird owners, although they wouldn't do that, should not handle your Sun Conure on the first day.

With these guidelines in place, you can also be assured that your family is also prepared for the bird. Try to tell them a little about Sun Conures, where they are from, what kind of behavior to expect and other things. A well informed family will always make it a lot easier for the bird to housebreak.

b. The First Day

The experience of being transferred from the pet store to a new home is not just difficult, but actually traumatic for Sun Conures. So it is best to leave them alone for a while. Especially when you are driving home, do not talk to the parrot. Your voice is new to them and alien, too. So, their stress just goes up tenfold.

Once you are home, open the enclosure, place the opening of the box or the carrier towards the opening of the enclosure and just wait for your bird to walk into his new home. This will take a few minutes. Also, this is when you will understand why a cat carrier or a smaller cage is a better option than a box in order to transfer the Sun Conure.

Gently close the door of the enclosure and just leave your Conure alone. Do not talk, tap the cage or just sit and stare at the bird. It is stressful for him. Instead, go about your routine. But, do not leave your house. He should be able to see you in the new environment. So, it is a good idea to choose a first day for the parrot when you are going to be home all day.

If you have a hand-bred bird, it is safe to interact with them after a few hours. Even this should be very gentle. You can place your hands on the sides of the bird's enclosure and just let him explore.

He may come and taste your finger. If he allows you to, stroke his cheeks and head with your finger. That way he knows that you are safe to approach. Then, you can say hello in a very soft voice. Keep the conversation on the first day limited and your bird will be able to cope.

Ask the breeder or the pet store owner for the favorite treat of your bird. Keeping this handy will actually help you reduce the stress of the Conure to a large extent. If you do not have bird food already, you can purchase some from your breeder or the pet store. This is the only preparation that you need to make for the first day.

If your Sun Conure is an aviary bird, it is best to leave him alone for at least two days. Your interaction should be limited to the feeding time. Remember that you never want to establish any dominance or submission with Conures. This can be done by maintaining your eyes at the eye level of the Conure every time you interact. Crouch down or step on a stool if you have to. That way you tell the bird that you are a friend or an equal.

c. How is the Bird's Behavior?
There are specific types of behaviors that new owners may not be prepared for. You will face problems, mostly with rescued birds or ones that are just at puberty. There are two most common behavioral concerns: aggression and fear. Both need additional care and can be frustrating sometimes. But these tips should help you get through that.

Is your Conure scared of you?

It is common for a Conure to be afraid of people. Sometimes, this is the result of past traumatic experiences and sometimes, it could also be due to improper socialization. The trademark behaviors of a scared Conure is nipping, biting at things or picking feathers constantly. Now there are several small things that can arouse this behavior in birds in a new environment. If they have never seen a moustache before, it can really freak them out. They can even be scared of a certain object that is too bright or large for them.

This is why you need to keep your Conure in an environment that is not noisy or bright on the first day. If the behavior persists even after clearing the environment, just let the bird settle. Leave some food and water and go about your routine. You must actually ignore your bird for two to three days and only interact when you feed him, but without making any eye contact. When he is settling in say hello softly but nothing more.

One thing you must never do is put the bird above your eye level. This makes them very aggressive and it is believed to be some sort of adaptive behavior from the wild.

Is your Conure biting?

There are various reasons why Conures bite. When they are new to an environment, it may be because they are stressed. The process of eradicating this behavior altogether is a long one and you need to go one step at a time. But, if this is your first day with the Conure, you must remember one thing, not to react to the nipping.

It may be hard to do, but do not let out a loud scream or do not say "No" to the Conure to stop them from biting. If you do it instinctively the first time you handle him, it is alright but never repeat this behavior. Screaming or saying "No" is actually a form of encouragement for the bird. They realize then that they have your attention. Then, they will not stop biting. In fact, they will develop different kinds of bites: want bites, attention bites and aggression bites. We will learn in detail about training your parrot to stop biting in the following chapters.

d. Building Trust

Parrots are highly intelligent creatures. You need to be aware of it at all times when you are interacting with your Sun Conures. It does not matter whether your Conure is pleasant in his behavior or even aggressive, the first thing that you need to establish is that you are comfortable in the environment that he is in. That means, you need to keep him in a room where he can see you walking around and just being yourself.

After two to three days, your bird should be settled in quite comfortably. That is when you can introduce treats to your bird. The best treat to start out with is some type of seed. You can try feeding it with your fingers. But, if you see that he does not respond or is scared of your fingers, you can give it with a spoon or maybe on a stick. When the bird begins to relish the treat, he will take it from your fingers too. If he still doesn't take it from your hand, just take the seed with your fingers and place it next to the bird. Then when he comes for the treat, praise him. Continue just this for about a week. When he is eating out of your hands comfortably, the next step is to let him out of the enclosure. It may take up to two weeks at the most to reach this stage.

Make sure that the wings of your birds are clipped before you let him out of the cage. If that is not what you want to do, you must establish a secure environment for the bird before you let him out. This is a checklist that you need to follow before you let out a bird without clipped wings at ANY time:

- ✓ All the windows must be closed with the screens pulled down.
- ✓ There should be no hot stove tops
- ✓ Close the lids of the toilets
- ✓ Keep all the doors shut
- ✓ There should be no new people the first time.
- ✓ You should definitely not have other pets around until they have had a chance to bond
- ✓ The fans should all be off

Allow him to explore the area around the cage. He may perch on the door or maybe on the cage itself. When he is settled somewhere comfortable, give him a treat. What you need to know about Conures is that they may not really leave the cage and go too far as they are inherently territorial. And when you put a treat into the food bowl, they will go back into the enclosure easily. If he does fly far, you can still lure him with a trail of his favorite treat. This is the initial stage of building trust that you need to work on before you get him to perch on your finger or on your shoulder.

e. Parrot Proofing

When you begin to let your parrot out of the cage, you need to make sure that the house is safe. This is very crucial if your bird's wings have not been clipped. Remember, even the ones with clipped wings are capable of some flight. The house should be safe for flight and you need to make sure that the bird does not escape or hurt himself. Here are some parrot proofing steps that you MUST take BEFORE letting your Sun Conure out of his cage:

- ✓ Don't allow any electrical wires to hang. These are perceived as perches or toys and the birds will go straight for them and may get severely injured. Put your wires into cable tubes. That way, your bird will not bite or tug at it.
- ✓ Have deadbolts on your doors. The birds may learn to open simple doors and may escape.
- ✓ Keep all the doors and windows closed whenever you are letting your bird out. That way, there are absolutely no chances of escape.
- ✓ If there are any pictures in your house that are hanging on the wall, bolt them into place. Your Sun Conure may try to sit on it. And, there are chances of the painting crashing down. If you have a bird that cannot fly well because of clipped wings, this is hazardous for the bird as well.
- ✓ Keep mirrors and your television covered if possible or train the bird to stop pecking at them. They may break it sometimes and hurt themselves.
- ✓ Keep the aquariums and toilet covers closed. Conures are not good swimmers and can drown in them.
- ✓ Nothing that the birds can get tangled in should be kept till your bird is trained. This includes things like wind chimes.
- ✓ Keep all your cupboard doors shut all the time. That way your Conure will not get trapped in them.
- ✓ Take shiny objects like chains out of blinds and other appliances in your house. That way you won't have them tugging and potentially dropping things on themselves.

✓ Light and breakable objects must be kept in safe places like a cabinet so that the birds don't tip them over.

✓ Anything that your bird may swallow like potpourri must be kept away.

There are some things that you cannot really avoid, such as gaps between or below furniture. Just keep an eye on the bird and ensure that he does not get trapped in these rather hard to reach areas. One way of taking care of this problem is by packing it with newspaper or more wood so that the bird cannot get in. Basically parrot proofing is almost like baby proofing. You need to think about everything that can go wrong.

f. Introducing your Sun Conure to other Pets

Choosing to allow your pets such as cats and dogs to interact with the birds or not is totally your call. Many Conure owners vouch that they are able to train their cats and dogs to live with the Conures successfully. However, in most cases, this only happens under supervision.

You have to understand that a Cat or a Dog is inherently a predator. That means they will always pose some amount of threat to your Sun Conure even after several years of interaction and living together. You may have seen pictures of birds and dogs or birds and cats playing with each other. This is certainly possible, but it may not be worth the risk.

You may have a cat or a dog with the most wonderful personality. They could simply love to watch birds and may be quite gentle, too. However, do not forget that they do have certain instincts. And, in most cases, it may not even be the instinct. It is the sheer size and strength of the other animal that poses the threat. In the case of cats, a lick or a bite can cause injuries and infections to the Conure. Even your cat may take in bacteria and germs. In case of a dog bite, it is usually fatal. This is because dogs have a higher bite strength that can just crush the Conure.

This should not stop you from introducing your pets to one another. They need to be aware of each other's presence. To begin with, if you have a home with pets like cats and dogs, make sure

41

that the cage you buy is very sturdy and has a lock that your pets or even the bird can't open easily. Never allow your pet, especially the cat, to perch on the cage. This makes the Conure react in the same manner as it would to a predator in the wild and they may never form that bond.

Never keep them in separate rooms. Make sure that your bird cage is in a room where the cats or dogs or both normally rest. That way they will interact and get familiar with each other. You must maintain this interaction until you see that your dog or cat has no interest in the bird. They shouldn't care about the bird's movements and must show no signs of curiosity towards the bird. When you know that your pets are comfortable in the presence of the Conure, you may try to take him out of the cage and bring him close to your pets. If your pets growl or snarl or try to lick the bird, stop them with a sharp, "NO!" That tells them that the bird is off limits.

The reason you need to keep them in the same room is that you do not invite any surprises. In case you left the cage door open and your Conure flew out, a dog or cat who is not familiar may attack him. However, if you have at least let them see each other constantly, the threat to your bird is lesser. In fact, some Conure parents have only realized that it is safe to leave their Conures and pets free and unattended by doing so accidentally. And, when they returned, they found that all the pets were in good health. But, never take this chance. Don't judge any pet by their personality first. This includes the birds. Remember always that they are creatures with a very strong predatory instinct that can be triggered in any way. Keeping your Conure in a safe cage when you are not around is the most recommended option.

g. Your Conure and Other Birds

If you have other pet birds, you need to make sure that you quarantine your new Conure before you introduce him to them. So keep the new bird in a separate cage. Even after you have taken him to a vet, you need to quarantine him for at least 30 days to make sure that he has no infections or health issues that can be passed to the other birds. Once you are sure of that, the next question is if you should introduce your pet birds to one another or not.

Let us start by understanding what situation the birds are in, whether they are from the same family or even different species. The wings of pet birds are usually clipped. So in the event of any confrontation between the birds, flying to safety is not an option. So the birds end up with no choice but to fight. It is for this reason that introducing your Conure to other birds, especially ones larger than them, can be tricky. In fact, most Conure or parrot injuries are related to other birds and not so much to pets like cats and dogs!

In addition to this, most birds, especially parrots, tend to treat their cages as their nests and can get extremely protective or territorial about it. So if you think that it is safe to place your new bird in the same cage as the other, you need to think again. Sometimes, you may have no problem at all. And, in other cases, you will discover that your birds just can't be the best of friends. There are some ways you can get your older birds to meet the new ones without creating much tension.

First, let us learn a little about bird psychology. Normally, birds like parrots will not fight in the wild. They only bluff one another by maintaining their posture as erect. But, in the mating season, they do get into physical fights, mostly attacking feet, beaks and eyes of one another. You may observe this sort of behavior only when one parrot or bird lands on the cage of the other. Remember that the other bird is very protective of the cage which is its current nest. So, the instinct will kick in and he will attack. When you are introducing the birds to one another, the ground rule is "DO NOT LET THEM GET ON EACH OTHER'S CAGE".

How do you do that? Here are some ways:

- Pay good attention to the birds in your house and note their reactions when you place their cages in the same room. Who is most aggressive? Has any of your older birds displayed aggression towards other birds?

- Start with individual introductions. If you have just one more bird, you will have to stick to just these. When you have multiple birds, you will have to take it slow and move on to the group introduction phase. Make the space neutral. Give them perches that are on the same level so that they do not feel any threat. Choose the least aggressive bird and introduce him to your new Conure.

  If they are quiet and not nippy, reward them and put them back to the cage. This way introduce your Conure individually to all your birds. If you see that one of them is being too aggressive and may chase or bite your new Conure, go back to the earlier steps and introduce them to each other in separate cages. You must do this until your Conure is familiar with the individual birds. That may take about a week or two.

- The next step is to try a group introduction. Let them all out of the cages and make sure you close the doors of the cages. That way, no bird will get back in and there is no chance of fights because of perching. You need to be in the room when this happens and just let them settle for a few minutes.

  If you see any sign of display, direct the aggressive bird back to his cage with a treat. These group introductions may take varying amounts of time to become easy for the birds. You must always supervise these introductions. Sometimes, it may take even close to three months to be sure that the birds are not aggressive towards one another.

- If you have an aviary, you can put your new bird in the cage with the others after these group interactions. This also requires a lot of supervision because the cage is not a neutral space for your new bird as the others, particularly a few, will show dominance in their territory. Even this interaction can be varied and the time taken to adjust to one another in this non-neutral environment extend to a few months.

- Once these interactions are calm, it is safe to introduce several perches and toys to the birds even in the presence of the new Conure. In case you see that your Conure is unable to get along with the old birds, even after a period of three months, just allow him to have his own cage. This is especially true when you have birds that have formed a strong bond with one another or even if you have a single bird who has formed a strong bond with you.

Conure Parent Tip: For other pets like rodents or ferrets, just don't let them out of the cage. Ferrets, especially will attack just about any animal or bird and are extremely tough predators. This is true for reptiles, too. If you have a fish tank at home, you need to keep it covered as drowning is a huge problem faced by Sun Conure parents.

h. Your Conure and Your Child

What is the one thing that is common between Sun Conures and Children? They both need a lot of attention! If you have a baby at home, it is a common Sun Conure parent advise to wait until your child is old enough to understand your instructions before you bring a Sun Conure home.

Are Sun Conures great with children? The honest answer is Not Quite. The thing is Sun Conures can be really curious. That makes them approach the child or toddler with much gusto! If this scares your child and the or she screams or runs, it makes the Conure jittery too. With repeated incidents like this, your Conure may form negative associations with your child and children in general. That makes them very agitated when they see children. They will even scream loudly when they see a child.

If you are expecting a baby, it is not the best idea to bring a new Sun Conure home. They need a lot of attention and will be noisy if you do not spend time with them. That will disturb your baby and will make your Conure very jealous of your child. A good idea would be if the dad or another member of the family bonds with the bird while the mom cares for the child. That way your bird gets the attention it wants and you have time for your baby too. These birds are safe to introduce to children. Let the bird out near the child after feeding or when he is sleeping. Give them treats and appreciate them for behaving well around the child. This is a good way to train the bird to stop being jealous of the child.

In case you have a toddler at home, the behavior of the child determines that way the bird will react to the child. If he is generally well behaved, your Sun can be quite friendly and gentle. But don't rush this. Allow your child to approach the cage with a treat. When the bird is able to accept treats from the child's hands, you can let them interact in the open.

However, if your child is naughty and loud, the bird is going to get scared. Things like shouting, poking and shoving treats in the bird's face are the kinds of behavior that will just get your Sun riled up.

In general, most Sun Conure owners maintain that these birds are not great for children. If you insist on getting a bird, bring a juvenile or baby bird home and let your child interact with him gently. Take it one step at a time and follow the same process that we spoke about in the "Building Trust" section.

After your Sun Conure gets used to the child, there is one type of behavior that is commonly noticed. This is especially true for Suns, who have been trained to perch on the shoulder or finger. They always go for the child's face. They will fly right over if they can or they will approach the face. This is not with an intention to bite or hurt the child, although it seems like that. All the Sun wants to do is perch on the head or the shoulder of your child. Teach your child to be perfectly still when they do this and you should not have any problem.

It is impossible to say that Sun Conures are entirely bad for children. It ultimately depends on the temperament of the bird and your child's approach towards the bird. Sometimes, the Sun Conures will form strong bonds with the children and get really protective about them.

The internet is flooded with videos of children and Conures being very close and friendly. I have seen one of a Sun Conure pulling out the loose teeth from a child's mouth without causing any pain. Well, it is a strange world. That said, there is no reason why you must not introduce your Conure to your child. Just be careful and patient and do not have unrealistic expectations from your Sun Conure.

If you have pets and children, you may want to do the introductions one at a time. First the pets, especially if they are birds. That way you will not have two animals that are under stress, plus a child or baby that needs attention. Make sure that your new Sun Conure is completely relaxed with your pets and then let them interact with the child. Until then, you may only want the child to approach the cage with treats or be with you when you are feeding the bird.

In the case of a baby, just make sure that your Sun Conure can see the baby in the same room. That way, they get familiar and know that there is another person in the family. Don't let the bird out of the cage around the child till he or she has settled in with the birds.

Once you decide if your pets like each other or not, you can decide if you want to keep them together or otherwise. Then, you get your child to actually interact with the Conure. Baby Conures and kids may grow up really well together as long as the birds feel loved and attended to.

Chapter 5: Sun Conure Care

Before we proceed into this chapter let us make a quick checklist of the things that you will need to provide good care for your Sun Conure:

- ✓ A good Housing Space
- ✓ A food bowl
- ✓ A water bowl
- ✓ Ornaments and toys
- ✓ Enough stock of Food
- ✓ Grooming Supplies
- ✓ Supplies to Clean the Cage
- ✓ Support from a Good Vet
- ✓ Pet insurance

We will discuss each one of these in detail to help you pick the best for your Sun Conure and keep him comfortable.

a. Housing your Conure

A nice cage makes a good enclosure for your Sun Conure and keeps them safe when you are away. Like we said before, the cage will become a nest for your birds. So, make it as comfortable and beautiful as you can.

How big should the cage be?

There is no limit to how large it can be. But there are some guidelines to follow for the minimum size of the housing space:

The bird should be able to spread his wings in all the directions.
He should be able to jump from one perch to the next.
He should be easily able to climb the bar
He should be able to play with the toys in the cage.

For a medium sized bird like the Sun Conure, you need a cage that is at least 24"X24"/30" in size. You need to ensure that the spacing of the bars is not more than 3/4th inch. This keeps them safe and prevents their feet or beaks from getting stuck.

What should it be made of?

When choosing a cage for your Sun Conure, there are two important requirements to keep in mind. The cage should be sturdy and it should have a very secure lock. Suns are highly intelligent and will learn to let themselves out if the lock is very easy. It is a good idea to get a padlock for the cage.

The best material for the cage is either stainless steel or any other metal that is powder coated. Avoid buying circular cages or the cylindrical ones, although they look very ornamental and pretty. A rectangular or square cage is ideal for the birds to move around freely. Ideally, you should be able to access the food and water bowl from the door of the cage. Or you will have to reach in every time you want to feed your bird. Some cages come with special openings that allow you to fill the food and water bowls quite easily.

Make sure that you never buy cages made of iron as it will rust. Of course, wood is not a good option as Sun Conures are chewers. They will make their way out before you even know it. You need to get a guarantee that there are no traces of led or zinc in the material used to construct the cage. This may lead to heavy metal poisoning, affecting the health of your Conure.

How can I furnish the cage?

There are several ornaments and toys that you can choose from to make the cage a fun place for your Sun Conure to live in. You can place lots of perches made from different material and of varying thickness. If you have more than one bird in the cage, the perches should be large enough and strong enough to allow them all to perch simultaneously. That way you will not have to worry about overcrowding and related aggression.

Place food and water bowls in such a way that they are free from droppings. Most often, bird cages will come with assigned slots for these bowls. Make sure that all the birds, in case of multiple pets, have access to food and that there are enough food and water bowls for all of them.

You can have many toys for your Sun Conure. Like we discussed before, these birds need a lot of mental stimulation that can come from these toys. You will find toys that are designed specifically for birds. Make sure you pick only those to ensure safety of your birds.

Conure Parent Tip: If you are looking for inexpensive toys for your bird, you can just roll some paper with treats and leave it in the cage. It will give your Conure a fun foraging activity. Besides that, you can also use paper cut in different shapes to entertain your bird!

Where to place the housing?

Birds are largely prey animals. So, you need to place your cage or housing in a place where they feel safe. Do not put the cage where predatory animals are in the bird's sight. Of course, once you introduce your pets, this will not be of concern. In fact, your household pets are not a problem because you are always around. But, if the cage is placed near a window from which the neighbor's large St. Bernard is visible, take care.

Never place the cage on the floor or right in the middle of the room. This makes the Sun Conures feel vulnerable and may put them under a lot of stress. You do not want them to be placed in a room where the noise from traffic is high. The best option for a Sun Conure Cage is against the wall in a position where the bird can get a full view of the room. If your Conure is very timid, you may consider covering a portion of the cage with a blanket or cover to give them an area that they can retreat to when they feel threatened.

Now, what you place around the cage also affects the health of your bird. Make sure you never leave cleaning supplies around the cage. The cage must not be near a vent or any place where you expect drafts.

Do you want to introduce new birds?

If you want to introduce a new bird or keep multiple birds in one housing space, here are some tips that will help you:

- ✓ All birds must have free access to food and water to avoid fights.
- ✓ For birds like the Sun Conure, each one requires at least 12 inches of perching space.
- ✓ Buy a cage that will allow all the birds to simultaneously spread their wings without running into ornaments or each other.
- ✓ If you notice any aggressive behavior, immediately separate the birds.

What substrate should you use?

Substrate refers to any material that you use to cover the bottom of your cage. These are usually absorbent material that can soak any droppings. At the same time, they should be safe for the birds in case they are foraging on the floor of the cage. The best option is newspaper or plain paper. Never use the glossy newspaper inserts as they may have some substances that are toxic for Conures.

You must never use sawdust, corncob, wood chips or wood shavings that are generally recommended for poultry. These materials soak up the droppings and feces and will have mold growing all over them in no time. This can lead to infections in your Conures.

It is a good idea to buy a cage with a grate just above the floor of the cage. This is good if you do not like the idea of your Sun Conures foraging through the messy substrate. If you do not have grates, pay special attention to the type of substrate you purchased.

Best food and water bowl options:

The best choice for food and water dishes are steel cups. These do not get scratches easily and are very easy to clean. It is important to ensure that the material is scratch proof as there can be a lot of bacterialgrowth in these spots, putting the birds at risk of infection. You can alternatively use ceramic bowls.

Water bottles are recommended by some Sun Conure owners as they prevent any dropping from getting into the food or water. The only problem with this is that it is hard to clean. In addition to that the cap and seal may develop mold, too.

There are several ready made feeders and water dispensers that you can buy from a pet store. These may cost anything between $8- $20. If you don't mind shelling out this much money, it is a good idea to invest in these feeders as they are usually designed to keep the food and water clean. Just make sure that the material that is used is safe for birds.

Keeping the cage clean

You must clean the cage of your bird once every day. The normal routine should include:
Disinfecting the food and water dishes after washing.
Changing the substrate.
Cleaning any droppings or dirt off the cage door, the bars, toys and perches.
Changing the dry food every morning, even if it looks good.

Besides this, you need to clean and disinfect everything in the cage at least once a month. Water must be changed twice each day for best results. When you are introducing a new bird, a thorough clean-up is a must.

The reason you need to clean so often is that the enclosure of the birds are actually small, confined spaces. There are chances that the droppings will accumulate on the perches and parts of the cage, and eventually grows mold or contaminate the water and food. This can cause severe infections in birds. That is why owners need to be additionally careful.

In order to disinfect the Conure's cage and toys, it is a good idea to use products like oxyfresh that are safe for birds. You can enquire with your local pet store if you are not sure about what products to use. Most of these are available in the form of sprays that can be used on the cage even when the birds are still inside. They are effective on the floors and the walls as well. They can be sourced at pet stores as well as some online forums that sell bird supplies.

Your Sun Conure is likely to chew and forage through the contents of the cage, including the bar and the floor. So, no matter what you use, you must be sure that it is not toxic to the birds. Avoid air fresheners or even certain bleaches as they are toxic for your Conures. You can only use very diluted Chlorine bleach in order to disinfect the food and water dishes only. You need to use a dilute of 1 tbsp per gallon to ensure that it is safe for your Conure. You need to make sure that these dishes are washed thoroughly to avoid any residues or remains.

Alternatively, some owners will use soap water. But this is only safe if you rise all the contents thoroughly with water. Soap may contain certain ingredients that will cause harm to your bird. Therefore, it is not recommended, but can be used as an alternative when you run out of the actual cleaning material that you use for the cages.

b. Feeding your Conure
Many first time owners are quite confused about what to feed their birds. There is a lot of contrasting information about what is good for your Sun and what isn't. So it can be a little hard. That

said, there are few things that are worth knowing about Sun Conures:

- They are not fussy eaters, but they pick their favorites.
- Overfeeding can make them gain weight.
- They need a lot of vitamins and calcium.
- The food consumed may increase during the breeding or mating season.

Getting the basics right

Conures eat a large variety of foods, including seeds, nuts and fresh fruits and vegetables. Some Sun Conure owners also give their pets eggs in small portions. If your Sun Conure develops a liking for this, you can even leave a small amount of the shell on as it is very good for the birds.

To begin with, you need to find a certain measure of the food that you are giving your Conure. It can take a while to get the exact amount in place and you may even have to do a few trials and errors to see how much your Conure will eat in one sitting. But, it is a good idea to go by tablespoon measures.

Pellets

The first thing that you need to give your Conure is dry pellets. Choose natural pellets from brands like Zupreem or Harrisons. If you choose the former, it can make up for 30% of your bird's diet but if you choose the latter, it should not be more than 10% of your bird's diet. The rest of it should contain fruits and veggies along with treats.

Avoid colored or dyed pellets as they may harm the bird. Pellets are made from crushed seeds and are full of fiber. They include a lot of vitamins and minerals such as calcium along with fruits and vegetables. These are all essentials in your Conure's diet. You can start the day out with these pellets and actually make them the base of the diet. You can give a Sun Conure about 2 tablespoons of dry pellets in a day.

Pellets are best stored frozen. Brands like Zupreem may spoil easily and need to be frozen. Pellets contain several nutrients and are hence a lot better for your bird than an all seed diet. Only seeds can cause health issues in the bird. Give the Sun Conure fresh pellets every morning. Remove the left overs and refill the food bowl every day.

Adding seed treats in between the pellets is a great idea and necessary for your bird's diet. You get seed treats like nutriberries that will add a lot of minerals and vitamins to the Conure's diet. Ideally birds as large as the Sun Conure will consume about 2 to 4 of these in the day. You can give them in between meals, ideally when they are half done with the pellets and once the pellets are fully done. There are other such treats as well that birds may like and you should be able to find them in any store. They are round and fun for the Sun Conure to eat as well as they let the bird forage a little.

Fruits and Vegetables

These are crucial parts of a bird's diet. Although some avian vets will tell you otherwise, many Conure owners will tell you from their personal experience that these birds need fruits and vegetables in order to stay as healthy as possible. Even in the wild, birds eat fruits and vegetables. So that is great for them.

You should ideally give a Sun Conure 1 tablespoon of vegetables and 1 tablespoon of fruits in a day. If you think that they will eat more, you must increase the vegetable portion. Vegetables give the birds a larger amount of Vitamin A that is essential for them. Fruits also give them the vitamins that they need, but also act as flavor addition to the bird's food.

In order to offer the fruits or vegetables, you can mix two or more varieties of each and heat them a little bit in the microwave, just to make them warm. Then, you may mash them and feed them to your bird. Now, sometimes birds may not develop any taste for these fruits and vegetables so you can add stronger flavors like strawberry or blueberry juice. These are great foods to include, but always remember that the portion of vegetables must be higher than fruits. Here are some good fruits and vegetable options for your birds:

Grapes
Apples
Pomegranate
Melon
Mango
Pineapple
Papaya
Kiwi
Watermelon
Star fruit
Blueberries
Cherries
Blackberries
Broccoli
Carrots
Beans
Sweet corn
Peppers
Spinach
Sweet potato
Butternut Squash
Red Cabbage
Beetroot
Sprouts

You can divide the 1 tablespoon portion across the day and feed them to your bird. You must offer this separately from the pellets and you will notice that your bird will pick his favorites. Offering seasonal fruits and vegetables can be great for your bird. But, before you introduce any new food to the Conure, ask a vet or do enough research to be sure that it is safe.

Calcium

Calcium is one of the most important minerals for your bird. Sometimes, your avian vet may recommend some supplements. Until such time, try to find natural sources of calcium for your bird. Pellets are the best option for a steady calcium source as most of them are fortified. You also get calcium perches and toys that the bird can enjoy and get his nutrients from.

Now just like us humans, birds need Vitamin D in order to synthesize the calcium. Sun Conures need full spectrum sunlight. So you need to take them out at least once a day for good sunlight. You can take the cage out if possible. If not, you get special transparent cages without filters that are safer and easier to use. If possible, place the cage near a good enough source of sunlight for everyday access. It shouldn't be too bright or hot, however.

What not to feed your birds

Peanuts: While other nuts like hazelnuts can be great for the Sun Conure as they are a source of high protein, peanuts can cause health problems because of fungal toxins.

Onions and Garlic: These two should not be offered in any form to the Sun Conures as they cause some irritation to begin with. In addition to that, they can make your Sun Conure very anemic.

Tomatoes: Tomatoes, especially raw ones, are hazardous to birds as they are acidic vegetables. They potentially cause ulcers in Sun Conures.

Mushrooms: They can cause serious digestive issues and even liver failure in Sun Conures.

Celery: If you can remove all the stringy part of celery, it is quite safe to feed to your Sun Conure. If not, it may lead to crop impactation.

Avocados: Avocadoes are poisonous to Sun Conures. They contain a certain toxin called perrsin that can cause breathing difficulties or even kill your Sun Conure in worst cases.

When you are uncertain of a certain food, be sure that you consult your vet or fellow Conure owners. When you are sure that it is of no harm to your bird, you can introduce the birds to it.

My Sun Conure hate Pellets

This is a common problem faced by Conure owners. Usually our birds come home from a pet store or from breeders. If they have been accustomed to a seed diet here, they may not take an instant liking towards seeds. Most Conures who are on a mainly seed diet will experience some health issues, the most pressing one being obesity.

One great way to introduce your bird to pellets is to include a small amount in the current seed diet. Then when he begins to eat that small amount, you may increase it. Keep increasing the proportion of the pellets till the seeds are completely out of the diet.

Another way to go about this is to give your Sun Conure mashed pellets. You can soak pellets in warm water until they are soft enough to crush. You can offer this to the bird and see if he or she eats it. If not, you can add a small amount of flavor inducer such as agave syrup, cranberry juice or even sunflower kernels to the crushed pellets. Make sure that you just add a tiny pinch of flavor that is enough to attract the bird, but not so much that it makes your Conure addicted to that flavor.

Whenever you are making a change in your Conure's diet, consult your vet. It is important to make sure that this diet change is not causing weight loss in your bird. Ideally, a Sun Conure adult should weigh between 100-130g. You can monitor this at home on a scale or you have to work along with an avian vet.

Conure Parent Tip: Sunflower seeds can be beneficial to your bird in very small amounts, maybe once a week. They do cause rapid weight gain but when given sparingly can be a great source of protein and Vitamin E.

Getting into a routine

The final question is how often should you feed your Sun Conure? Ideally feeding the bird twice with a few treats in between can work really well. So in the morning offer the pellets first. Then at about 11 am, you can give the bird one serving vegetable. Then in the evening at about 4 pm, you can give him the portion of fruits. Now in between these meals you may offer seed treats like nurtiberries. Establish a routine with your Sun Conure to ensure that he is eating on time.

Also measure the amount of food per meal to make sure that your bird does not over eat. You will know that your bird is done eating at a given meal time when he shows loss of interest in the food. Offer him only this much per sitting to avoid overeating. Only the pellets can be made available all day. That should also be done in controlled proportions of 2 tablespoons a day. Replace the water in the dish regularly as Conures may dip their food in water and mess it up.

c.   Grooming your Conure

Keeping your Conure looking good is definitely your responsibility. But grooming has more to it than just the looks. It helps your bird stay free from infections. With good grooming practices, you can also make sure that your bird stays safe and looks great. Unlike dogs and cats, birds don't need elaborate baths. There are other aspects to grooming your Sun Conure that you need to keep in mind.

1.   Bathing your Conure

Conures inherently like to stay clean. They have several instinctive cleaning methods in the wild. You need to be able to provide the one factor that the birds miss, which is rain, through a regular bath. Now, as you know, Sun Conures are from tropical parts of the world where rainfall is common. So, that is essential for them to stay clean. Besides that, they have three natural ways of keeping their bodies free from any dirt:

Powder down: This refers to a small amount of dander or powder that the birds produce from the feathers. All Sun Conures have certain down feathers that continue to grow for long periods of time. These feathers have very fine extensions that break often. This powder coats the feathers and the body of the bird. This powder repels water and dirt. It sticks to the dirt and when the bird preens itself, falls down with the dirt. The more dander the bird produces, the healthier he will be. Of course, this is not a welcome instinct for most pet Conures.

Preening: This is the healthiest natural grooming method for the birds. It is useful to scape feathers and keep them moist. You will see your Sun Conure uses the water from the bowls to preen himself. Besides that, preening ensures that all the feathers of the bird are in place and can be used properly. In the wild, parrots of any kind will not let one feather go out of place because it makes them more vulnerable to predator attacks. A feather sticking out means that the predator will be able to spot the bird in a flock.

When they preen themselves, these birds also break a certain gland known as the Preen gland or the Uropygial Gland that is present just at the base of the tail. This gland produces a certain oil that the birds rub all over their feathers just to make them water proof.

How to bathe your Conure?

If this is the first time your Conure is taking a bath in your home, you need to make it a pleasant memory for him. Sometimes, when they have been bathed very harshly in their younger days at the breeders' or at the pet store they will develop a negative feeling towards bathing. They may scream and rant when they hear the sound of a water tub filling up.

In order to give your Conure a bath, just fill up a small bird bath or even your sink with water and lead the bird to it. You can use toys or treats to do this. Allow them to stand at the edge of the sink and just explore. They may be excited, but scared to get into the water.

In order to lower the Conure into the tub, allow them to perch on your palm and slowly lower it towards the water. Then let the bird step in. In about ten seconds of entering the water tub, the bird should become familiar with or just used to it. Keep on talking to your bird and make him feel safe. Praise him when he is wading in the water. You can also put some of his favorite toys into the water.

If you need to use soap, it is safe to use any mild human soap or shampoo. But, it is recommended that you buy specially made soaps to avoid any sort of allergy or infection. You can make a diluted soap solution and use your hands to give him a lather. Take a lot of care to avoid getting any into his eyes. In case of thick dirt, you can use a wash cloth or a very soft toothbrush to gently brush it off. Then rinse the bird well with clean warm water and use a towel to pat him dry.

Some Conure owners use hair dryers to dry their birds. But it is recommended that you let the bird dry naturally as this gives them a chance to even preen their feathers into place. Of course you need to make sure that the A/C and the fans are off in the room where the bird is drying himself off.

For fully grown Conures, a bath is not necessary. You can simply spray some water on them or just allow them to walk around under the shower. You will get special shower perches in any pet store that allow you to place the perch on the tiles of the shower wall with suction cups. Avoid using soaps during showers as your bird may not allow you to get it all off. They will only stay under the shower for a few minutes and fly off. This is just to make up for their instinctive love of the rain.

You can give your Sun Conure a thorough bath every fortnight. A shower is recommended twice in a week to keep the bird healthy and free from any infections. When you are putting them in a bird bath, make sure that it is very shallow as parrots are not good swimmers as a general rule. It should just be enough for the bird to soak himself.

2. Trimming the Toe Nails and Beak

Do not try this on your own the first time. You will need to get some advice and tutoring from your vet before you try to trim your bird's beak and toenails at home.

Beak trimming

While the beak may seem like a hard and easy surface to trim, you need to understand that the exoskeleton goes all the way up to the brain of your Sun Conure and any damage caused to this can be very serious for the bird. Also, most birds will hate beak trimming and will resist it. So, you need to learn about this as much as you can and try it out with an expert guiding you the first few times.

To start with, you need to comfort your Sun Conure first. Hold it close to your chest and stroke the head and cheeks till they are settled in. Then gently hold the head with one finger and put your thumb on the underside of the sharp edge and try to get the mouth open slightly. Then you can file the back of the beak with a soft nail filer. All you want to do is get the tip a little rounded. Do not make it blunt. The beak is an important part of the Sun Conures movements and will affect play and perching, too.

You will only have to trim the beak if you notice any overgrowths. This prevents them from getting it stuck to the toys or even certain fabric and getting injured. Otherwise, the beak needs to be sharp to help the bird pick foods, climb, perch and play. So, just make the edge slightly rounded and not flat and blunt. Keep filing small bits and check the edge. When you are sure that it feels less pointy, you can stop.

Trimming the Toenails

Now you may wonder why toe nail trimming is necessary at all. This is done not to protect yourself but to actually protect your bird. You see these birds will perch on your shoulders or on the furniture and may get their sharp toe nails stuck in some of the netted or woven fabrics. And, when they try to fly away, there are many instances when the whole toe gets ripped off or the legs get displaced from the hip socket. This is true as birds are extremely delicate creatures. Trimming the toe nails prevents these types of ghastly accidents.

To trim the toe nail, just hold the bird on your thigh and cup him down in place gently. Hold the toes with your fingers while the palm is holding the bird down. You can even do this on a table if you are more comfortable. Only when you have a good grip on the bird should you try to file the nails.

Place the file on the back of the toenail and keep trimming the nails till the needle sharp tips to become rounded. Every time you are done with one toe nail, allow the bird to rest for a while. If he gets too jittery and restless, a treat may be a good idea. When your bird is calm and playful, proceed to the next toe nail. This process is quite stressful for the bird and you need to take it slow and easy. Be patient and keep praising the bird as you go through with the filing process.

Toe nail and beak trimming should be done once every 3-4 months. This is an important grooming practice for the safety of your bird. However, if you are not very good with handling your Sun Conure and have not established a strong bond with him yet, you must not attempt to do this by yourself as it is a very difficult process for the birds. The sound of trimming, the feeling and the fact that you are dealing with the parts of the body that are meant for protection can register as danger in the bird's mind.

3. Wing Clipping

To make sure that your Sun Conure does not fly away or escape, wing clipping may be a great idea. But, this is a very tricky process and must be done only by an expert. If you are new to Sun Conure parenting, do not attempt this alone. You may just want to watch and learn for a couple of months and have your avian vet train you to clip the wings at home. You can seriously injure the bird as there are several capillaries and blood vessels running to the wings. You need to know exactly how much to clip without causing any bleeding or injury.

You only have to clip the primary feathers that are the longest ones and closer to the bird's body. Doing this will not render your bird flightless but will not allow them to get a lift in their flight. That way, they will stay closer to the ground and stay out of trouble.

To begin with, take a small towel and roll the Sun Conure over. Put the towel over the bird and hold him down gently. Then, from the open end of the towel, extend one wing at a time and spread it open. This is what you need to do if your bird is not used to clipping or if you are inexperienced. It will prevent sudden movements that may lead to clipping of the blood feathers.

You need to keep a Styptic Pencil ready. This is used to clot blood when people have accidental cuts while shaving. It works really well on birds as well. You should be able to get this in any supermarket at the personal care section or in your local pharmacy. Wet the end and keep it prepared for any accidents.

Birds molt and therefore their feathers keep growing back. You will recognize new feathers, as they are in a sort of casing. You do not want to cut these feathers as they will bleed profusely.

The longest feathers, usually the first 10 are the primary feathers. You might want to start in the middle at about the third feather and cut the ends of three or four feathers from there. The reason for this is that the first feather and the last feather of the wing are the last ones to be replaced in the molting process. This means that they could still be blood feathers that are vulnerable.

Spread your bird's wings out one at a time. Hold the feathers that you want to cut with your finger and trim about 1 cm with a sharp pair of scissors. Don't snap the scissors. Cut it very gently to make sure that your bird does not get scared and flinch. Do the same on the other side making sure that you have cut the exact same amount on both sides. Birds need their wings to be equal for any sort of balance.

When you are done, hold both the wings out to make sure that they are equal. If you hit any blood feather accidentally, you can just dab the end of the cut feather with the Styptic pencil to take care of it. Give your bird a treat at the end of the clipping section to give him some positive association.

Now, if you go to an avian vet, they may pluck the entire feather out instead of just clipping it. This may be a better practice as birds tend to chew on the wings that have been cut. This could lead to infections or further damage to the wings. This should be done ONLY by a veterinarian.

If you have pets that are predators such as cats and dogs, make sure that your bird can fly to some extent. That way, they are able to flee in case of any untoward incident. Otherwise, they will be trapped and can get seriously injured.

Conure Parent Tip: Even when your Conure's wings have been clipped, be very careful outdoors. While they may not be able to get any lift indoors, you can't say the same when they are out. They can get a lot of assistance from the wind if it is slightly stronger and CAN fly away. That means you lost your pet, but it also means that this bird who cannot fly perfectly is out in the wild, unable to protect itself from predators. For the safety of your Conure, avoid letting them out in the open without any cage or enclosure.

4. Helping Molting Conures

Molting is a common behavior pattern exhibited by birds. In Sun Conures this behavior will start at the age of 8 to 10 months. They will shed their feathers and grow new ones. In juveniles, this is when they get rid of the green feathers and grow the bright yellow ones.

When your Conure is molting, he or she will be very irritable and nippy. This is not a good time to try to discipline them or teach them new tricks. They may want to be left alone for a few days till the cycle is over. Conures molt once every year, usually in the warmer months. They don't shed all their feathers and become bald, however, as most new owners expect. They first shed the innermost feathers and move outwards. This molting period will last for close to a week.

You can help your Sun Conure deal with this itchy and irritating process by spraying some water on the feathers. Give them foods that are very rich in proteins such as almonds and make sure clean water is always available to them. Another thing that you can do is preen the feathers using a soft toothbrush if your bird is comfortable being handled. That will ease a lot of irritation and soothe the bird. You have to be really gently as the new feathers are really delicate and may also be painful.

d. **Finding a Good Avian Vet**

This is the first thing you need to do. In fact, it is a good idea to get in touch with an avian vet in your locality before you actually bring your pet home. For the initial checkup, your breeder or pet store will be able to recommend someone. However, if that is not within easy access from your home, you need to look for one. While regular veterinary clinics may be able to handle emergencies for you, an avian vet will be able to handle and complications in your bird's health. He will also be able to guide you with specific requirements and behaviors of the bird.

There are some shocking statistics about pet bird owners and veterinarians. Research shows that between 60% and 68% of cat or dog owners will take their pets to be examined by a vet. However, only 7.6% of pet bird owners will go to an avian veterinarian. In an event that the bird is unwell, they take the bird back to the pet store or to the breeder! [*Pet Age Magazine, 1989*]

While things may be a little better today, some bird owners still do not find a specific avian vet to treat their birds. Any medicine from a pet store will only help mask the condition but will never cure it entirely.

So, what is an Avian Vet?

Veterinarians often specialize in one species or type of pet. While most often they are taught to deal with common pets like horses, cows, dogs and cats in vet school, exotic pets are studied separately as an elective. An individual who has studied birds, including the exotic ones, is called an avian vet. They would also have to spend several years practicing in facilities that deal with these birds specifically.

Veterinarians who specialize in specific rare species are part of the Association of Avian Vets. Since the Sun Conure is not a rare breed, you don't have to specifically look for a vet who is part of the AAV. It is, however an advantage if you find one who is.

Finding an Avian veterinarian

The first source would be your breeder or the pet store. You can try the recommended vet, but do not just assume that he or she is the best for your pet. In fact, many breeders and pet stores may have tie ups with the veterinarian in order to void your health certificate.

The best sources to get information about avian vets in your locality would be:

✓ Online or local bird clubs
✓ A regular veterinarian's office
✓ Good and reputed pet stores.

However, the best source to find avian veterinarians is the Association of Avian Vets. You can log on to their website www.aav.org or call the Central Office in Florida on (407)393-8901. They also have an active page on most social networking sites that can help you even find fellow Conure owners in your locality.

It is worth knowing that some avian vets may also treat other exotic creatures like reptiles and amphibians. This does not make them unreliable avian vets or less informed in comparison to those who deal only with birds. Of course, you can ask them how much of their practice is dedicated to birds to make sure that they have enough experience with handling them. In case they are handling just up to 2-3 birds in a month, you can ask them to recommend someone who deals with birds mostly.

You can even casually ask your vet about interesting avian seminars in your city. They should be informed about this if they are interested in learning and educating themselves about birds. A good avian vet will probably attend a few himself.

The next most important question is whether they are available 24/7. If not, what would they recommend in case of an emergency in their absence? Then you also have to do some research about the hospital they recommend. If the avian vet you are meeting does not have this back up, look for another one who does.

How to know that your Vet/ Hospital is inexperienced?

It is not enough that your vet is educated about birds, even his support staff should be fairly informed. There are some signs that will tell you if your Avian vet hospital is really experienced or not:

- When you call for an appointment, they will tell you that it is too cold to bring your Conure out instead of telling you how you may keep him warm on the way.

- The staff does not know what type of bird you have. They should definitely be able to recognize a Sun Conure as it is such a common pet.

- The staff is afraid to handle the birds, especially baby birds.

- Your vet examines the bird through the cage. He should do a correct physical exam to check your bird properly.

- The vet does not measure your Sun Conure. This is the first thing they need to do.

- They will not discuss basics like the bird's diet with you. Most avian problems are related to malnutrition and the first thing a good veterinary hospital does is find out all details about that.

- The appointments are not longer than 15 minutes. A good examination will take at least 30 minutes. So, if they are simply scheduling appointments every 15 minutes, they are probably not doing a thorough job.

- They do not recommend annual check-ups. If the hospital tells you that you need to bring the bird in only when there is a problem, you need to show concern.

Basics of a good facility

Take a tour of the hospital or clinic to see how well the place is equipped. Here are some basics that are definitely available at any serious Avian Vet facility:

A gram scale to measure the weight of the birds accurately.

A good diet for the birds who have been hospitalized, including pellets, fruits and vegetables.

Incubator cages

Separate rooms for the birds if they are also dealing with other animals like reptiles or even cats and dogs.

Once you have found a good vet

A good veterinarian is your most important support system in dealing with your Sun Conure. Stick with them always and make sure that you follow their instructions with respect to your bird to the last letter. If you are not cooperative, the help they can provide is very limited. Of course, you can call them about concerns you have about your Sun Conure but don't make this a habit. If you want to discuss something, fix an appointment.

e. Insurance for your Sun Conures

Getting pet insurance for birds is not very easy. Most insurance companies will provide policies for cats and dogs, but rarely for birds. However, there are some reliable ones that will give you decent benefits. The most common things that are covered by popular pet insurance are:

Veterinary charges: They will pay for certain diagnostic procedures like X-rays and even some consultation fees. Veterinarian costs will most include emergencies only. In case of birds like the Sun Conure that have long lives, there may be a limit on the cover offered annually that may go up to $1500 or £3000.

Escape or Loss/ Death: If you lose your bird to theft or death, they may cover some amount of the market value of an exotic bird. Theft and Escape cover requires you to fulfill some security conditions such as purchasing a five lever lock for the cage door.

Public Liability: This covers any damage caused by your bird to another person or property.

Overseas covers: This is necessary for you to travel with your pet to some countries.

The cost of your insurance with all these covers will come up to about $150 or £280 a month. These covers are purchase separately and you can cut costs on things like overseas cover or public liability cover if you do not think that it is necessary. However, all these covers are highly recommended for all pet owners. You can compare the costs of various insurance plans online to find one that works for you. If you have multiple birds, some of them may also offer a 10% discount on the insurance cover.

The two most popular insurance plans for these birds are:

Pet Assure: With this policy, you can only have your bird checked by a vet in the network approved by them. If your vet is not part of this network, you need to find one that is or you will not be able to get the cover for vet costs.

VPI: This insurance does allow you to see any preferred veterinarian. However, they do put a limit on the number of visits and the cover that they offer annually. So, you may not be able to get full coverage for any major procedure that your bird may have to undergo.

That said, there is no policy for birds that is perfect. So, if you want to choose the most reliable one it may be the one that your veterinarian is associated with. That way you can be assured of some cover at least.

Most pet Conure owners will suggest that you alternatively, open a savings account for your Sun Conure. This is primarily to be equipped for medical emergencies. In addition to that, some may even tell you not to get insurance as it may be too expensive and may not even give you as many benefits. In fact, these insurance premiums can be more expensive than the ones that you have for human beings! However, if you have any travel plans in the future with your Sun Conure, then getting insurance might be mandatory in some countries.

Chapter 6: Bonding with your Conure

Bonding in reference to birds refers to the relationship that is built with a potential mate. So, if you have a pair of birds, they will bond and not get so attached to you. However, when you bring home a single Sun Conure and are trying to form a bond with him or her, you need to realize that there is only one thing to bonding with Sun Conures, and that is trust.

If you can establish with your bird that you are a friend and are not looking at harming or causing any form of stress, then you are able to build a bond with the Conure. This is a slow process and you must let the bird take their time to actually get used to you.

Be Predictable

The first thing that you need to introduce to a bird's mind is predictability of your behavior. Now, you are a strange species to your bird and they will not trust you immediately. After all, you are larger than them and in the food cycle the birds are prey animals. So, never rush in.

For the first few days, you must only keep the bird in a room where they can see you and your whole family and observe your behavior. A simple routine like saying help or goodbye every time you enter or leave the room will make a big difference. A feeding routine will also give the bird something to predict. Feeding should be done by one or two members of the family. It is best that only one person does this, preferably the owner. Know that Conures do not bond with everyone and will pick just one member of the family or at the most two. They may be social with others, but the bond will remain with one person.

Once you have established this predictability, you can go back to Chapter 4 and work on building trust. This chapter tells you what you need to do in order to make your bird willing to come out of the cage. When you know that your bird is comfortable outside the cage, you can begin the next part of trust building which is the Step up Training.

a. Step up Training

Step up training is the best display of trust towards the owner. Now, not only does the Step up training form the basis of building the relationship, it is also one of the most important things to teach your Sun Conure. In case of any emergency, such as a fire or a natural disaster, you should be able to reach in and have the bird step up on your finger in order to escape. If you do not train the bird to step up, he may not let you handle him and pet him either. That makes it very difficult to do the other fun things like teaching him tricks and generally including him in various activities throughout your day.

Your hands are very scary for a new Sun Conure. Also, their cage is their home. When you just intrude and put your hands through, you are most likely to get bitten. So take it as slow as you possibly can. You will need a lot of treats that you can feed them with your hands if they are comfortable or with a spoon or a stick. When you have successfully taught your Conure to come out of the cage, you are ready to have them step up on your finger.

The first thing to do would be to lead them to the open door of the Cage. Then, you can offer your finger like a perch just a few centimeters away from the door. Remember to hold the finger horizontally so that it looks like a branch and do not point at the bird in such a way that your fingers look like food to them.

Then, hold the treat behind the perch finger. At this point, they may immediately step up or may hesitate. Do not stress them too much. Offer the step up command about two to three times and if the bird only looks at the treat and does not come for it, put the treat back in the food bowl and try again.

It is also possible that your bird will put his beak around your perch finger and gently nibble. They are not biting and you mustn't ever draw your hand back. In the wild, birds do this to make sure that the perch is steady. So, if your bird bites your finger and you hold it still, he will probably step up. But if you draw the finger away, he will lose trust in your finger.

When he climbs up, offer him a treat. Let him stay for a while and put him back in the cage. Offer him a final treat before closing the cage door. Keep doing this for a few days. Place your perch finger, say "Step Up" and when he does, offer a treat. At one point just the step up command without the treat is good enough. Remember to praise your bird abundantly irrespective of whether he makes progress or not.

After you have taught the bird to step up on your finger, you can offer your shoulder as the next step. You will do the same thing, hold the bird up to your shoulder and when he steps onto it, offer him a treat. That way you can lead him up to your head as well. Getting the bird on your shoulder is great progress as it allows you to include him in all your daily activities. You can keep him on your shoulder as you fold laundry, do the dishes or even just sit down and read a book. That way, he will feel like you are giving him attention and is likely to bond faster.

Once you have established the trust to get the Sun Conure to step up onto your finger, you can try to pet him. Start by stroking the head and the cheeks. If he allows you to do that, you can move on to the critical part which is touching the beak. If your Conure allows you to touch the beak without biting, then it means that he has established a high level of trust in you.

Conure Parent Tip: When you are teaching the Sun Conure anything new, whether he is learning to come out of the cage or onto your finger, you need to spend at least 15 minutes every day doing so. You need to keep the time of training and the place of training consistent for better results.

b. Taming a Sun Conure

There are two issues that you will face with a Sun Conure. The first one is biting and the other one is screaming. Sun Conures are very noisy birds and can really get on your nerves sometimes. Well, that is their way of seeking your attention and actually communicating with you. You need to be flattered if your Sun Conure is noisy around you as he is only trying to talk to you. But if this screaming is incessant and high pitched like he is scared, you need to start taming him.

Dealing with Screaming

Screaming will always be a part of a Sun Conure's life. Especially in the mornings and evenings, calling out or screaming is normal. You need to be prepared for this as a pet parent. The only time when the screaming becomes a problem is when your Sun Conure begins to scream every time you leave the room. That means he is only screaming for your attention and nothing more. So, here are a couple of things that you do not want to do when you observe this behavior:

- Do not scream back at the bird or say, "Stop" or "Don't Scream".

- Do not come running back into the room every time just to get him to stop screaming.

This encourages screaming. When you respond with your own voice or by coming to the bird, you are doing exactly what they want. You are their "Flock" that is calling back when they call. So they are happy to have your attention and will continue to scream. Unlike dogs or cats, a sharp "No!" is actually not a negative thing for birds. They think of it as your call in response to theirs.

Instead, it is a good idea to put some toy or treat in the cage before you leave the room. That way they have something more interesting and something to distract them. It tells them that you are going away means that it is time for some fun inside the cage. The next thing you can do is just let the bird scream and not come back. Wait for the screaming to stop and then go in and reward your bird. That way the bird understands that you will come back when he is quiet and will also reward him. Eventually, the period of silence will increase. Some people will tell you to put a blanket on the cage when the bird screams. While this works, it is negative reinforcement. Hence, I would discourage it.

Dealing with Biting

Biting stems out of two needs- defense and attention. However, biting of any king must be discouraged. The bird must know that it is not acceptable behavior. Also, if you are able to build trust with the Sun Conure, biting will significantly stop. There are other things that you can try to stop your bird from biting.

In the initial days of your interaction with your Conure, biting only comes from fear. So, you need to be patient. If your bird bites you when you are trying to get them to perch on your finger, you have to remember not to shout or scream. The moment you do that, the bird gets a message that this is how they can control you and stop you from doing what they are not fond of. Instead, you just let the bird back in the cage and try again.

The next thing is when your Conure has started perching on your hand, but begins to bite when you are trying to pet it. That is when you have a little more trust with the bird. Then, you should gently push the head down with your index finger. It is a small and slight push that should not hurt the bird. Then in a very soft voice say "No biting". Then attempt to pet the Conure again till you have a positive reaction. Just stroking the cheek is good. When this happens, praise the bird for being good, put the bird back in the cage and give him a closing treat. At this stage, the bird finds the cage to be a positive reinforcement.

The last type of biting that you want to discourage is want bites. This is when you have established a good relationship with your bird and he nips at you when he wants something that is in your hand. For instance, if he is on your shoulder and you have a fruit in your hand, he will bit your ear or cheek. There are two things that you can do.

First, you can just return the bird to the cage. This stops the behavior as the bird wants to be with you at this stage and going back to the cage is not as much fun as being with you.

The next thing is to shake his balance. If he is on your head or shoulder, you can actually run or jog. That puts the bird off balance and will make him release the beak. If he is on your finger, you can gently shake your hand or simply raise your elbow. This will put him off balance and make him release the beak. Now losing balance is something that Conures hate and will give up any behavior that leads to it.

c. Understanding Conure Body Language

Your Sun Conure will use body language to communicate with you. He will also use different types of calls that you need to learn to decipher when you are forming a bond with your Sun Conure. Let us talk about the vocalizations first and then go to the visual communication through the body.

1. Vocalization

Sun Conures are extremely vocal birds and will rely on their voices as an effective means of communication. There are some trademark sounds that your Sun will make to tell you how he or she is feeling:

- **Talking, Whistling and Singing:** This means that your bird is happy and content

- **Chattering:** The most commonly used method to get your attention. This is seen in birds that are still learning to talk.

- **Clicking the tongue:** They are just having fun or are asking you to do something fun with them.

- **Low growl:** This is a sign of aggression and shows that something is troubling or threatening the Conure. Look for objects that your bird dislikes and get it out of their sight. Never handle a growling Conure.

2. Body Language

A Sun Conure will use his eyes, beak, head, wings, tail and feet to communicate with you. Here are some of the most commonly observed physical displays or visualizations in the case of Sun Conures.

Beak

- Grinding the beak shows that your bird is satisfied and is ready for some rest.
- He will tug on your shirt collar with his beak indicating that he wants to get off or go back in the cage.
- He will lower his beak to the ground or floor of the cage to show you that he wants you to scratch him.
- This is a disgusting one, but very endearing. A parrot will regurgitate in front of you as a sign of affection. In the wild, they regurgitate food so that they can share it with their mate!

Head:

- Bobbing the head up and down indicates that your pet is very happy or excited.
- If your Conure lowers his head and turns it by 90 degrees, it means that he sees something that he wants.
- If he bobs his head and regurgitates, then you have been an excellent Conure parent, congratulations!

Tail

- Wagging the tail is a sign of happiness and excitement. It means he wants to play with you.
- If the tail bobs up and down it is the sign of strenuous activity. This is how birds cool off. If tail bobbing occurs even when the bird is at rest, it is a sign of some illness.
- Tail fanning is the bird's attempt to look bigger and scare away a potential threat. It is a display of aggression.

Feet:

- If the Sun Conure paces up and down the cage or on the perch, he wants to come to you.
- If he stands fully straight, he wants to come to you.
- If he scratches the floor of the cage, it means that he wants to get out of the cage. Do not give into this behavior.
- Tapping the foot on the floor of the cage is yet another sign of aggression that you simply must not ignore.

Wings and feathers:

- Ruffled feathers show that the bird is unwell or cold.
- Quivering wings is a sign that the bird is ready to mate.
- Flapping the wings is an attempt at getting your attention.
- Flapping the wings on the other hand means that he is in pain or is agitated. If he also hunches his shoulders when he does this, he is deprived of attention or is really hungry.
- Drooping wings in older Conures is a sign of an illness.

When you begin to understand the body language of your Sun Conures, you will be able to predict their behavior and eventually make your bond stronger. Once you are confident that your Sun Conure is not afraid of you, the next step is to start training him or her. This book will cover some of the basics. You have several resources such as online videos that will show you different tricks that you can try with your bird. The trick to all forms of training is the same. All you need to know is that with higher levels of difficulty, you need more patience.

d. Training your Sun Conure

Sun Conures and parrots, in general are extremely intelligent creatures that can be trained to perform a variety of tricks. Just as you would with any other pet, you will start with gaining trust. Then you can start from simple commands and move over to the more complex ones.

1. Potty Training a Conure

The first thing to do is to establish with your bird that pooping the cage is alright. That way, they will not hold it in when they are in the cage and you are away. A small Conure like a Sun Conure will poop every 10 to 15 minutes and if you want to avoid accidents when your bird is out of the cage, you need to potty train him.

The first thing to do would be to teach him to poop inside the cage in the morning. So when they are up, put a paper on the floor of the cage and wait for the bird to poop. They will show a very distinct type of body language which is usually lifting their tail and leaning down on the perch. Then, when they do poop, praise them abundantly and offer a treat such as a nurtiberry which is part of the diet.

The next step is to watch for these signs after you have taught your bird to step up. When you see the pooping body language, hold them over a trash can or over a piece of paper. Then when they do poop on that, they need to be praised abundantly. That way, they know that there is one place or appropriate place for them to poop and they will not mess the whole house up.

2. Teaching Your Conure to Talk

Conures are not capable of learning too many words. They may learn up to 10 words in their lifetime. So you need to choose what you want to teach them. Sun Conures don't really learn the meaning of words, but only learn to mimic you. They will associate it with a particular action, if you say the word before that action like a command.

So, pick a word that you want to teach him. Suppose you pick, "Goodbye", you need to say this every day at a specific time. Make sure there are no distractions like TV sounds when you are saying the word that you want to teach him. Now associate that with an action that he will remember like you walking out of the room. Say it in a high pitched sound and sound as excited as you can. If you are super excited, he will feel motivated to learn that call as it is positive to him. Eventually, when you go out of the room, he will respond with a high pitched, "Goodbye". Be patient.

3. Teaching him to lay on his back

This is a step up to more advanced tricks. You need to try this when your Sun Conure is okay with being touched and petted. This is a strange thing for the Conure to do and if he resists, be patient.

- Start by getting him to perch on your finger.

- Then, rest your finger on a flat surface.

- Place the hand that is free on his back to support him and lean forward. Say, "On your back" or any such command in an excited voice. At one point he will be laying with his back on your hand.

- Now, shower him with praise and tell him how smart he is. You can give him toys and just play with him by tickling his tummy. He will learn to associate being on the back with positive experiences.

- You need to give him the same surface to practice all the time and lean forward a little.

- Then, the gesture of you leaning in also reinforces the habit and he will learn to lie down on his back.

Teaching a Sun Conure tricks can be a lot of fun. They will really appreciate the time you spend with them. You can play several games with them like peek-a-boo or even rolling a toy back and forth. Sun Conures also love to dance. They will respond to rhythm and music with a lot of enthusiasm. So if you play music and just sway your hips and move to the rhythm, your Sun Conure will respond with similar movements immediately.

This is a lot of fun. And, you can expect several surprises from your birds such as learning to say words you never intended to teach them! That is the best part about having a Sun Conure. They are highly intelligent, making the bonding experience so unpredictable and exciting at the same time.

Be assured that these kind of mental stimulants will only make your Conure healthier by the day. He will learn to associate with you as a great companion and friend.

Chapter 7: Sun Conure Breeding

Some Sun Conure breeders will tell you that they breed all year around. That is not quite true. The most prominent breeding season for Sun Conures is when the temperature increases and the sunlight increases, which is typically in spring. Some of them may even become hormonal in summer. If you have a pair of Sun Conures- a male and a female, you need to know that they might mate and that you may have to be prepared to raise the babies and take care of the brooding female. The usual age of maturity for Sun Conures is about 2 years.

a. Will your Sun Conures mate?

Just having a pair of Sun Conures (one male and one female) does not guarantee that they will mate. Sun Conures are monogamous birds. This means that they will only mate with one partner in a lifetime. So, for the Suns to breed, they need to like each other. If you see favorable behavior such as preening the feathers of each other, sleeping next to each other, locking beaks almost like they are kissing and just staying together all the time, you can safely say that you have a nuptial bond between the birds. A sign that these birds are mates is feeding each other. They are likely to mate during the breeding season.

To encourage breeding, you need to watch their behavior closely. If you notice the male mounting the female, you need to ensure that they get some peace and quiet. Sun Conures will not breed if there is any interference such as noise from television, human voices or any disturbance from the pets. You can change their current enclosure to a special nesting cage that is placed in a quiet room. Remember, Sun Conures will not show specific breeding or mating behavior like other birds. This is true for most birds from the Conure family.

b. Setting up for Breeding Season

Sun Conures are shy birds and will need a specific nesting box if they need to be encouraged to breed. You need to get a large nesting box that is at least 18 inches deep or more. This is basically to make sure that the nesting material, usually something soft like pine shavings, is available in plenty. Sun Conures tend to keep kicking this material out and if the nest is not deep enough, there are chances that the amount of pine shavings available will not be enough when the eggs are laid.

You can use a wooden nesting box. However, Sun Conures tend to be chewers and may damage the box. So a metal one is more suitable. The idea is to have a nesting box that can last for several breeding seasons. You see, Sun Conures prefer the same nesting box year after year.

This box can be placed at a high position in the cage. If you have a special nesting cage, you can place it there. Remember that height is an important factor for brooding hens to feel comfortable.

In case your bird does not have enough access to light, you may have to set up infrared lighting that you need to turn on at about 4pm and turn off by about 10pm. You need not increase temperatures in the case of Sun Conures.

c. What to feed a Brooding Conure?

After mating, if the female spends most of her time in the nesting box, it only means that she is brooding. The diet of the brooding Conures should be really nutritious to avoid common problems such as egg binding which can be very painful and sometimes fatal.

You need to give your Sun Conure fresh pellets, lots of fresh fruits and vegetables and even some cuttlebone to ensure that she has a good source of calcium. Ensuring that your Conure is getting enough calcium can be a challenge, but it is very important. You can give them additional treats like raisins, almonds, walnuts, egg shells and even mineral blocks that are added to the water. Make sure that your bird gets good sunlight in order to utilize the calcium that you are providing her with.

Your vet should be able to help you with supplements that you can mix in the food or water of your Sun Conure.

d. Signs of Egg Laying

You should watch your Sun Conure's behavior closely to make sure that you know when she may lay eggs. You will see some obvious signs like eating more from the mineral block or chewing from the cuttlebone. She will also become very cranky and noisy. She becomes very territorial and is a little aggressive as well. She will start seeking your attention and will want you to accept annoying behavior such as nipping at your shirt or biting. Do not encourage that. She will also develop a bald patch on the belly, which is called the brood patch. This is to help her pass heat from her body to the eggs.

When she is ready, she will lay the egg in the nesting box and will incubate it for about 28 days when provided with nesting conditions such as toys, sunlight and a lot of attention. Some Conure owners will just leave their pet alone as soon as the eggs are laid. This makes the female actually lose interest in the eggs. They believe that you do not care about them because of the eggs. This kind of behavior is displayed when the Conure owners do not want the eggs to hatch.

Each clutch will have between 3 to 8 eggs. The hen lays one egg each day. It is possible that the first clutch is infertile.

Conure Parent Tip: If your Sun Conure loses interest in the eggs for other reasons and you do not want the eggs to be damaged, you can bring home an incubator. This is an expensive piece of equipment.

e. Raising the Baby Conures

Raising the chicks is a lot of responsibility. Most often, pet owners just leave the Sun Conure pair to raise their hatchlings who will arrive after about 28 days of incubation. The parents will feed the babies for 8 weeks and really care for them. Now, you have three options when it comes to rearing the baby Conures:

1. With the Parents
Sun Conure chicks grow really fast. If you do not disturb the hatchlings and just leave them in the box, then the parents will raise them. At about 4 weeks, these babies will develop pin feathers. When they are 8 weeks old, they are fully weaned at the age of 8 weeks.

If you interfere ever so slightly with the parents, you will have to take up the responsibility of raising the chicks. This is a lot of work and definitely not for someone who has no experience. You can watch as the parents feed and tame their young just like in the wild and it is a fascinating sight. Allowing the hatchlings to be hand raised has several advantages. To begin with, it is more economical. Second, these birds are likely to make better breeding specimens.

2. Hand Raising the Chicks
Some Sun Conure owners may want to hand raise the chicks to build a good bond with them. It is also true that these baby birds make amazing pets. You must not take the baby out of the nest immediately after hatching. It is a good idea to leave them there until they are at least 4 weeks old. These babies will believe that they are human beings when they are raised by people. They will

start to preen your hair, cuddle up towards you and even give you gentle nips or kisses.

The older the chicks are when they are removed from the nest, the stronger they are. This makes them easier to handle and less susceptible to infections. Once they are out you need to start hand feeding them. Now, there are special mixes called hand rearing formula that you can buy at any pet store. These formulae are rich in nutrients and will help the babies grow healthy.

Follow the directions for heating as mentioned on the box. The chicks need their food to be at a certain temperature in order to process them properly. You also need to feed them the number of times recommended on the box. There are at least 3-4 feeding cycles in a day, separated by a few hours.

3. Co -parenting

You may also choose to work with the Conure parents and raise the chicks with them. This means that the Conure parents will also be a part of the raising process. You will take turns between the feeding cycles and the babies will be removed from the nest to hand feed at least once a day.

Co-parenting is only possible when you have a very trusting relationship with your birds. If they can accept your attempts to take the babies out as assistance and not acceptance, then you can do this. Your birds need to be extremely calm to allow you to co-parent the chicks. Otherwise, they will develop aggressive behavior which they will direct at each other. The male may attack the female or they may even kill the hatchlings. You must back off if the birds show any signs of resistance.

However, if the birds accept your assistance, it can be a wonderfully rewarding experience for you. The responsibility is reduced on your part and on the part of the Conure parents, the babies are more social and tame and the parents still have the pleasure raising their own young.

It does not matter how you choose to raise the birds. Remember that all the experiences are equally rewarding. You may choose to add these birds to your flock. That is, however, not a practical thing to do as Sun Conures that have mated once will do so every year and the babies have a life span of 30 years or more. So, it is a good idea to find these babies loving homes when they are a few years old.

In case you find the first experience with the chicks very taxing, you can discourage breeding by disallowing ideal nesting conditions as mentioned above. Some pet Conure owners also avoid raising chicks because they find it very hard to part with them.

Chapter 8: Travelling with Sun Conures

New pet owners may take travelling with pet Sun Conures for granted. It is not as simple as strapping the travel cage in and just driving off. Birds can get very stressed in long car drives and you need to make sure that you get your Conure accustomed to the experience if driving around with the pet is necessary. If your vet is a little far away from your home, you need make sure that you help your Conure enjoy the drive. Or else, every visit to the vet will be a nightmare!

a. Driving with your Sun Conure

It is recommended that you get a separate travelling cage for your Sun Conure. This is a smaller cage that is easier to carry around. Make the Conure like this cage by adding toys and perches and leading him into it occasionally with some treats. That way, he knows that it is a safe place to be in. He also need to feel like it is a positive place to be in.

The next step is to introduce your Sun Conure to car drives. If you know that you may have to take the bird on long car journeys, either to visit the vet or because of an impending move, you need to prepare him for this.

The Drive

First transfer your Sun Conure to the travel cage. Then place the cage in the car. Before you do this, ensure that the temperature of the car is at room level. You may have to turn the heat up or down depending on the season. Too much heat can cause heat strokes and too much cold will stress the bird unnecessarily.

Leave the cage in the car for a few minutes and take him back home. Spend a week to just get him accustomed to sitting in your car comfortably. He should display very normal behavior and must not seem perturbed. Then, you can move to the next step which is the actual drive.

For the drive, place the cage in the back seat and strap it in place with the seat belt. Take a small drive down the block and see how the bird reacts. If he is whistling and normal, you have a bird who likes to travel. On the other hand if he gets distressed and sits in a corner of the cage, shivers or vomits, it means that you need to be more persistent.

You need to make the idea of coming into a car fun for the bird. That includes talking to him when you are driving, praising him for staying calm and offering him a lot of juicy fruits like pineapples that are not just tasty but also hydrating for your bird. Eventually, your bird will start accepting the car as a neutral and fun space. Then you can increase the length of the drives. For long drives, make sure that you have enough substrate on the floor, plenty of access to fresh water and some treats that he enjoys.

If you have to move houses

When you are moving, you will have several bags in your car while you are driving. This is also stressful for a Sun Conure. So, you need to add one bag at a time and continue to take him on drives. You need to do this till you are able to place all the bags in the car along with the bird cage and drive without stressing the bird.

The reason you need to add the bags one at a time and really plan for a move is that the color, shape and size of the bag can be scary for the birds. If you can plan well, you will be able keep the stress levels low not just for the bird but for yourself too.

When you are ready to move, make an appointment with your avian vet for a final examination that renders your Conure fit to travel. Make sure you get all the medical records of your Sun Conure from your vet to be able to share it with the new one.

Housebreaking into a new home will not be as stressful for your bird because you are around. Still, give them time and appreciate their need to be left alone and soak in the new environment.

b. Finding a Sitter

You may want to travel to a different state or country with your Sun Conure. This is a big step if you are moving out as you will have to check the laws regarding bringing the bird into another country. Some countries have very strict quarantining measures. So if you are planning a move, you need to make sure that your Sun Conure will be able to come with you. If not, you have to change your option of travel or you may have to take the hard way out by finding a new home for your Sun.

But, if you are only travelling temporarily on a vacation or for a business trip, taking your bird along is not recommended. It is a better idea to leave him in a place that is more familiar to him. This can be under the care of a relative, a pet sitter or even in a facility that may be provided by your own avian vet. For a temporary trip, it is not really worth putting your Sun Conure through so much stress.

Finding someone to care for your Conure

The best option is to keep your Sun Conure in your home and request your friend or relative to take care of the bird. They should be entirely trust worthy. This is the best and most reliable option. However, if you do not have someone you know who can take care of your bird, you can always hire a pet sitter.

There are several professional pet sitters who can follow your routine and exact care while you are away. You can look up the yellow pages, ask fellow bird owners or check the internet for options. Two of the most reliable sources to find pet sitters for your Sun Conure are National Association of Pet Sitters or www.petsitters.org and Pet Sitters International or www.petsit.com.

As per the National Association of Professional Pet Sitters, here are a few guidelines that you can follow to find a good pet sitter:

- Look for a sitter who has some commercial liability insurance. These are bonded sitters who can be held responsible in case something goes wrong with your pet.

- Make sure you have enough references from past clients. You can also ask the sitter to connect you with them. If there is any hesitation, you may want to reconsider.

- You need to get a complete written description of all the services that they will provide including the fees.

- You need to meet the pet sitter once. Ask them to visit your home and discuss all the services in complete detail.

- Be observant when you are interviewing the sitter. Are they comfortable with your Sun Conure? Ask him if he owns birds and also about the experience that he has with sitting birds.

- You need to make a written contract if you decide to use the services of a particular sitter. The most important thing is to check for his or her arrangements with veterinarians, in case your bird falls sick or there is any emergency to find out how he or she is going to deal with it.

- If the sitter herself or himself falls sick and is unable to care for your bird, is there any replacement? If so, meet that person.

In case you are not comfortable with the idea of leaving the bird with a sitter, there are several boarding options. The best one is with your avian vet if they provide those services. If not, you can ask them to recommend a suitable boarding for your pet Conure. Make sure you check the conditions of boarding and that your bird will be safe from any infections during this time.

Air Travel with Sun Conures

In case you have to take your bird on a plane for whatever reasons, it is a process that you have to plan very carefully. If not done properly, you could be putting the health of your bird at risk.

Know the laws

There are several wildlife laws in order to protect certain species of animals. Now, as you know Sun Conures are considered endangered and there may be several laws that make it hard for you to take the bird out of your country or even out of your state. There are three laws that you need to thoroughly check before you make any overseas plans involving the Sun Conure:

1. Convention on the International Trade in Endangered Species of Wild Fauna and Flora (CITES)
2. Wild Bird Conservation Act
3. Endangered Species Act

These laws have been enforced to ensure that these birds are safe and not illegally transported or traded. You can check the websites of these laws to see what laws are in reference with your Sun Conure. You may even take the assistance of your Avian vet in determining whether travel to certain countries is possible with Sun Conures or not. You may have to apply for special permits that will allow you to travel with your Pet Conure. It can take up to 60 days to process these permits. So, you need to plan well in advance. You have to check these laws, even if you are only crossing state borders.

Once this is done, the next step is the actual plane travel which can be a traumatic experience for your Conure. Here are some things that you need to do to make sure that air travel is hassle free:

- Talk to different airlines and understand their regulations about transporting pets. Now, with birds, the airlines will have specifications about how long the bird can stay in cargo. If your flight is longer than the time given, you may have to break your trip down to various transits. If switching planes is necessary, make sure you do not have to switch the airlines. This means you have to learn a whole new set of rules.

- Then, get a carrier as per the guidelines of the airlines.

- 10 days prior to the air travel, you need to get a health certificate from your avian vet. If you are travelling overseas, you will have to get this certificate signed by the USDA and the Animal and Plant Health Inspection Service.

- You need to take a CITES permit with you when travelling overseas.

- Make sure that your bird is strapped and harnessed in case his wings have not been clipped. In case of long flights, it is recommended that you have the bird's wings trimmed.

- You must carry enough food supplies with you for the whole trip. In the travelling cage, make sure you have enough food available for the bird. You can also get a water dropper to keep the bird hydrated. The substrate should be increased to make the flight comfortable for your bird.

After you have all this in place, you can travel with your Sun Conure. Remember that it may take a little settling in after flight journeys. These journeys are extremely stressful for the bird and can make them anxious. If you notice any unusual behavior in your Sun Conure, make sure that you have him checked by an avian vet the moment you are able to. There may be stress related problems or even breathing issues that your bird may develop on long flights.

Make sure that you are gentle with your Conure and that you let him know that you really appreciate his cooperation during the flight. You cannot take pets in cabins as you would know. So always thoroughly check the airlines policies and even ask fellow bird owners about their experiences with different airlines and choose one that you can truly trust. After all, you do not want him to be dumped in the back of the cargo like baggage. He should be able to travel comfortably at the very least and airline personnel should handle your pet Conure with lots of care.

Chapter 9: Common Conure Health Issues

Like all birds, Sun Conures are susceptible to several diseases. These diseases are usually related to nutritional deficiencies and some could also be stress induced. You need to be able to identify that your bird is under the weather in the first place. Here are some sure shots signs that your Sun Conure is unwell:

✓ Resting too often
✓ Poor appetite
✓ Opening and closing the beak frequently
✓ Staying at the bottom of the age
✓ Reduced water intake or sudden increase in water intake
✓ Growth around the beak
✓ Loose droppings
✓ Sudden weight loss with the chest bone becoming visible
✓ Cloudy eyes
✓ Discharge from nasal cavity
✓ Ruffled feathers
✓ Lethargy
✓ Drooping wings

If you see these signs, you could take your bird to the vet immediately as a preventive measure against impending health problems that can be serious.

Conure Parent Tip: Loose stool or water dropping may even occur when you have fed your Sun Conure fruits. Strongly colored fruits and vegetables can also alter the color of the poop. So, unusual droppings, while a sign of concern cannot be the only symptom of illnesses in Sun Conures.

a. Common Sun Conure Illnesses

The first thing to know about the most common Sun Conure illnesses is that they are airborne. So all the precautions that you may take to keep your bird free from illnesses can be futile. So, what you need to do is always keep yourself updated about Sun Conure health and diseases in order to be prepared for any emergency. Here are some of the most common health conditions observed in Sun Conures:

Pacheco Virus Disease

This is highly contagious and is caused by a type of herpes virus that is found in South America. This is one of the top causes of Sun Conure deaths. This condition causes quick liver damage that can even kill your bird. The symptoms are not very apparent. In the initial stages, you will observe very brightly colored vomit that may be yellow or green in color. When the condition is terminal, you will see neurological problems in the bird. Sometimes, birds could just be carriers of this virus which is why quarantining new members of the flock is very important.

Remedy: There is only one known oral medicine called Acyclovir that you need to administer every 8 hours. This medicine is very expensive and will be detested by birds. Sadly, most treatments are not effective because the damage caused is so rapid.

Beak and Feather Syndrome (PBFDS)

This condition is spread by dried droppings and feather dust. You will see that the bird shows abnormal development of new feathers. After molting, the feathers that develop will look really swollen and messy. The beak that is normally shiny will begin to look very dull and covered in feather dust. Abnormal growth of the beak is also a symptom associated with this condition. If allowed to progress, PBFDS can lead to paralysis in the bird and also cause death.

Remedy: This is a condition with no cure. It will eventually cause death in Conures. Sometimes, the birds are also put to sleep or just isolated. In some cases, it has been observed that the birds develop immunity naturally over a period of time. Then all the symptoms will disappear and the bird goes back to a normal life. This is possible with continued care and good nutrition.

Wasting Disease

This disease is common to almost all species of Sun Conures. It is very contagious and can stay dormant for several years. This condition affects the nervous system of your bird. The impact is quite severe, causing tremors, paralysis and also seizures in the bird. Usually, it leads to cardiac arrests that are fatal to the birds. There are no cures for this condition. However, when you Conure has been diagnosed with this condition, it is possible to prolong his life by including lots of supplementation in his diet. Choose supplements that are easy to digest in order to help your Sun Conure out. The final outcome of this condition is death and there is no preventive measure as it is a viral infection that manifests suddenly.

Papilloma

This is yet another viral infection, but the good news is that it is not fatal. You will see signs of infection near the mouth and the throat of the bird. You will see a wart like growth that develops in this region. You need to have these removed immediately. While the infection itself is not fatal, the growths can block the nasal passage or the throat and cause death by choking. The growth keeps increasing in size, leading to several physiological conditions if not treated on time.

Remedy: The best remedy for this condition is to have the infected area treated. The growth can be removed using a laser surgery.

Psittacosis

This is another viral infection that is also known as Conure fever. The bird is affected at any age, although the younger ones are more susceptible. The less mature the immune system, the higher the chances of infection. This condition is caused by a strain of Chlamydiosis virus. The symptoms associated with this condition include pneumonia, conjunctivitis, nasal discharge, incessant sneezing and lime green droppings that indicate liver and kidney malfunction.

In higher stages, this condition may even lead to seizures, tremors, paralysis and other neurological issues.

Remedy: The common drug that is administered is tetracycline. A medicine called doxycycline is widely used these days. This medicine can be given through an injection or orally. Usually the course of this medicine lasts for 45 days. Keeping the cage sanitized can improve healing. Remember that this condition is also contagious to human beings leading to pneumonia or fever. You need to wash your hands every time you handle the bird or its belongings and even wear a mask while doing so.

Gout

Any calcification in the kidney leads to gout. This condition usually affects younger birds that are around 4-8 weeks of age. It is usually caused by an improper amount of calcium in the food. This condition is completely diet related and can occur in birds who have a lower rate of metabolism. The first few signs are not very obvious. There may be slight dehydration in the birds along with vomiting. These signs are similar to any bacterial infection. However, getting a blood test done when you see these symptoms is advised.

Eventually, you will see the skin on the chest shrink and the bird will be unable to retain any food or fluids.

Remedy: Keep the birds hydrated always. Colchicine and Allopurinal are recommended to remove all the urates from the body.

Conure Pox

All species of Conures are susceptible to this condition. It is caused by an avian pox virus infection. This infection can be spread by any insect or from one bird to another. The most common signs of the condition include discharge from the mouth, eyes and gullet. Depigmentation occurs along with abnormalities in the roof of the beak. These scars will compromise on the appearance of the Conure, actually leading to depression in some birds.

Remedy:

You need to give the bird high amounts of Vitamin A, preferably through injections. Antibiotics will be administered by the vet. If the bird stops eating, you may have to force feed him to get best results. Sometimes, he just may be too weak to eat. Any mucous in the eyes or nasal passage must be cleaned using a prescribed washing solution. Otherwise, these deposits may harden and cause damage to the body parts. Allow the scabs to stay once they have formed to protect your bird.

Aspergillosis

This is a condition that affects the lungs of the bird. Symptoms like cough, fever and chest pain are common with this condition. Aspergillosis is caused by the Aspergella fungus that usually grows in the dark and damp areas. This is a sign of poor sanitation.

When in its acute form, this condition leads to dysponea, anorexia and sudden death. Congestion of the air sacs leads to strained breathing, lethargy, white colored mucuous and depression in the birds. In case the central nervous system is affected by this condition, it leads to paralysis.

Remedy: Two of the most commonly recommended medicines are intraconozole and fluconazole. You can also ensure better sanitation to improve the response to medication.

Salmonellosis

This is one of the most serious infections in avians. It can lead to death and most birds are carriers of this bacteria. Even in the acute stages, this condition can be treated. However, this is not enough as the bird may become a potential carrier of the disease. Breeders will not treat these birds and will just allow them to die as they pose a lot of threat to the other birds.

Remedy: Screen any new bird for infection. If one of your Conures is diagnosed with Salmonellosis, keeping him isolated is possibly the best remedy to prevent the infection from spreading. The bird can be given recommended antibiotics in isolation.

Conure Parent Tip: Salmonella can cause serious infections in humans too. If you have birds of any kind at home, all members of your family must wash their hands thoroughly before eating. It is recommended that you wash your hands immediately after handling the birds.

Sinusitis

In Sun Conures, this is a very common respiratory problem. When you bring home a Sun Conure, always have the medicines for cold and any respiratory infection within easy access. The cause of this condition is not known. However, it is very contagious and requires immediate attention. One organism that is suspected to cause this condition in birds is Mycoplasma, although there is no confirmation for this.

Remedy: Sinusitis is followed by secondary infections usually, making treatment complicated. The best way to control this condition is by providing high doses of Vitamin A. If the bird does not respond to this, consult your vet.

Nasal Discarges

This is very common in Sun Conures who are not getting enough Vitamin A in their diet. You can reduce the symptoms of this condition by increasing supplementation and by increasing the quantity of food. It is very important to give your Sun Conure a balanced diet to prevent any health problem.

Conure Bleeding Syndrome

This is another common disease that is commonly seen in Sun Conures. It is believed to be caused by a certain strain of retrovirus, although the exact cause remains unknown. Another theory is that this condition is caused by Vitamin K deficiency.

The initial symptoms are very similar to heavy metal poisoning which includes obvious discomfort and uncharacteristic screaming. The most significant symptom is bleeding from the mouth and nasal cavity. If left untreated, this condition may be fatal for Sun Conures.

Remedy: Injecting Vitamin D3 and K1 are the most effective remedies for this condition in Sun Conures.

b. Preventive Measures

Disease prevention in pets is only a matter of establishing a healthy environment for them. Some of the best preventive measures include:

- ✓ Quarantining new birds to ensure that there are no contagious diseases.
- ✓ Providing a balanced meal that is rich in Vitamins, especially Vitamin A and minerals like Calcium.
- ✓ Making sure that clean drinking water is available to the bird at all times.
- ✓ Give him a lot of mental stimulation through toys and games. Sun Conures need a lot of attention.
- ✓ Make sure that he has access to enough sunlight and this may be full spectrum sunlight every day. Take him out into the porch and let them soak the sun in for a while.
- ✓ Keeping the cage, food and water bowls clean.
- ✓ Grooming the bird and keeping him clean.
- ✓ Regular visits to the veterinarian. It is recommended that you have your bird checked every 6 months to 1 year.

With all these measures, you should be able to prevent most infections and illnesses that may affect your Sun Conure.

Dealing with Common Injuries

Your bird is susceptible to several accidents at home or even because of some social aggression. You need to be prepared to take care of the most common injuries that are seen among pet birds

Broken wings: Hold the wing close to the body of the bird and strap it in place using gauze. Then, rush your pet to the veterinarian.

Bleeding or Cuts: Bleeding from the beak, wing or the feet requires immediate attention from the vet. However, if you are dealing with a broken blood feather or a mild gash on the body, use a Styptic pencil to stop bleeding and leave the wound alone for a while. Make sure you slowly wash off dirt if any before applying anything on the wound. In case of profuse bleeding, hold the wound down with gauze and tie a bandage around it. Then take him to the vet immediately. You must take the bird to a vet to ensure that there are no infections.

Ruptured air sacs: This is a condition that will usually heal on its own. However, you need to provide some assistance to the bird to allow the air to escape from beneath the skin. A vet will make an incision and insert a tube to let the air pass. This tube is removed once the air sac heals. The incision will close in a few weeks.

Conure First Aid Kit

Any evident injury needs professional care. However, you need to have a first aid kit to help provide immediate relief to your Conure. Some essentials in the first aid kit are:

- Flour: This is very effective in controlling bleeding without increasing blood pressure
- File: To keep the beak and nails trimmed
- Tweezers: Usually bird bandages and tapes are tiny and need tweezers to hold them easily.
- Cotton swabs: To control any bleeding and to clean any pus or blood of the bird.
- Gauze: Use sterile ones to stop bleeding in open wounds.
- Bandage material: To control bleeding, hold the wing in place when it is broken, etc. Make sure that you get a bandage that won't stick to the Conure's feathers.
- Toothpick: To remove any debris in the nostrils.

- Disinfectant: Hydrogen peroxide is the best option to clean a wound. This is the only thing you can use without the vet's recommendation as long as you keep it away from the eyes, mouth and ears.
- A small syringe: this will help you wash off the wounds.
- A towel: To restrain an injured bird.

This is the basic kit that you must always keep handy to ensure that you are able to provide immediate medical help to your Sun Conure whenever necessary.

Chapter 10: Costs of Keeping a Sun Conure

Now that you are aware of all the care that your Sun Conure needs, let us take a look at the monetary responsibility that you will be taking on by bringing a Sun Conure home.

- Cost of the Conure: $200-400 or £100 to 250 depending upon the age, the breeding conditions and the source that you buy them from.

- Cage: $150-400 or £80-200 depending upon the features available and the size. This is a one time investment and it is recommended that you get the best.

- Food: $40 or £25 every month.

- Toys: This really depends upon the type of toys that you buy. But you will shell out a minimum of $15 or £10 on each toy that you buy.

- Wing clipping: If you get your wing clipped outside, then you will spend about $15 to £10 every four months.

- Veterinarian Cost: You will spend at least $50 or £30 per visit to your veterinarian. You can expect annual costs of about $1200 or £650 per year.

- Pet Insurance: Depending on the kinds of covers that you are getting, your pet insurance may cost anything between $150-280 or £80-150 every month.

In all, you need to keep aside a minimum of $450-500 or £200-250 every month to provide proper care for your bird. You must never make any compromises in this respect and ensure that your bird gets the best life.

If you have any doubts about being able to support your bird, wait for a time when you know that you can give him or her better care. That will make the whole experience with your Sun Conure more fulfilling instead of causing unwanted stress and irritation.

Think ahead and make your budget plans for at least five years before you bring a Conure home. In case you see anything in the future like a marriage or a baby that can increase your financial responsibilities, see if your Sun Conure would fit into it too. The expense is one of the biggest factors that causes owners to give up their Sun Conures. This can be very traumatic for the bird and, indeed, very bitter for the owner.

So, it is best that you make a good budget that may even include a few savings for your Conure every month to help you deal with any emergency.

Conclusion

Now that you have made your mind up to bring a Sun Conure home, here are a few questions that you must ask yourself to be sure that you are willing to make a commitment for almost 30 years to your bird:

- **Does a Sun Conure match your lifestyle?** If you are someone who is travelling frequently or is working long hours you need to think this through. Who will take care of your bird then?

- **How is your home environment?** Your home should have enough space to house a Sun Conure. Also remember that this bird is fairly noisy. So it is only courteous to consider what your neighbors think. If they have problems with the noise, how can you make your space sound proof? Always ask your landlord before you bring home a pet to avoid any nasty surprises for either of you.

- **Why do you want a Sun Conure?** If you thought that birds are easy to take care of, you know better now. If you still insist, ask yourself why? If you are someone who likes to interact with birds and play with them, the Conure may be the pet for you. However, if you are only looking at having a pretty bird in your home, you may not want to make this commitment.

- **Do you have kids?** If yes, can you manage both the Sun Conure and the kids? If you think yes, then go ahead. If not, you can wait until your children grow a little older and then bring home a Sun Conure.

- **What is your life like right now?** You need to be in good health, have a steady source of income and have fairly pleasant relationships in your life to be able to commit to a bird. If you are in a place in life right now when you are not sure if you can devote attention to the Sun Conure, wait a little longer. If you are too stressed already, you do not want an additional responsibility.

- **Is 30 years alright with you?** What do you think your life will be like in 30 years? Will you have the same enthusiasm towards the bird? It is a long commitment and you really need to be well prepared to take it on.

- **Can you meet all of your Sun Conure's needs?** There are several expenses involved with Sun Conures including veterinary costs, food and other small things like toys. Can you afford that? Will you be able to keep your bird healthy? Besides that, you should also be able to fulfill your Conure's need for attention.

Once you are confidently able to answer all these questions, you can be sure that you can give a Sun Conure a wonderful and loving home.

Thank you for downloading this book. I hope that it was able to give you all the information that you need about raising healthy Sun Conures. Here is wishing you a wonderful journey of love and adventures with your beautiful Sun Conure.

References

Seek to continually learn more about Sun Conures. As with the care of all exotic pets, new techniques, strategies and concepts in such areas as housing, diet, health care and breeding are discovered and implemented at a rapid rate. Never turn down an opportunity to learn more about your new pets, and eagerly seek out those who may know more than you do about these fascinating birds.

1. Websites

In the information age, learning more about your sun conures is only a few clicks away. Be sure to bookmark these sites for quick access in the future.

Important: At the time of writing, all the following links were active and functional; in the event that any source should re-direct you to an inactive page, please understand that the maintenance of these websites is subject to Internet-policies and the preferences of the website owners; we cannot claim personal responsibility for the same.

Informational Websites

www.myconure.com

www.birdsnways.com

www.lafeber.com

www.parrots.org

www.downhomepets.com

www.voren.com

www.parrotforums.com

www.beautyofbirds.com

www.stuff4petz.com

wwwe.n.allexperts.com

www.bookyards.com

www.parrotsecrets.com

www.greencheekconure.net

www,animal-world.com

www.parrotsdailynews.com

w11.zetaboards.com

www.petpeoplesplace.com

www.readyforpets.com

www.reptile-parrots.com

www.forums.avianavenue.com

www.kellyvillepets.com.au

www.parrotfeather.com

www.zoologica.wordpress.com

www.fantasticpetcare.co.uk

www.birdchannel.com

www.petbirdpage.com

https://www.youtube.com/watch?v=HSyhFv_U2Rk

https://www.youtube.com/watch?v=uoRlawwdobA

https://www.youtube.com/watch?v=osfSpYYe0HA

https://www.youtube.com/watch?v=osfSpYYe0HA

https://www.youtube.com/watch?v=WPfusxS14Yg

Published by IMB Publishing 2016

CPSIA information can be obtained
at www.ICGtesting.com
Printed in the USA
BVHW08s2115060618
518373BV00007B/216/P